INTERNATIONAL AUDITING

International Auditing is a major contribution to the literature on international auditing. Aimed at both practising and academic accountants, it will also be of interest to financial managers and directors who deal with auditors and to all users of audit reports, such as investors and lenders.

The book describes the auditing standards that exist in the specially selected countries of Australia, Canada, France, West Germany, Japan, the Netherlands, the UK and the USA, and places these standards in the context of these countries' national auditing and accounting environment. It examines a number of issues that arise in the audits of multinational companies, and looks at the important topic of international harmonisation. There is also a chapter which looks at the rankings and structure of the international auditing firms.

Although there is a considerable literature on international accounting, there is relatively little on international auditing. The growing professional and academic interest in international aspects of auditing and accounting will be well served by this thorough, up-to-date survey by a practising auditor.

Leslie G. Campbell is an accounting research manager with Deloitte Haskins & Sells. He was educated at the University of Glasgow and holds a master's degree in international financial management. He has been involved in a number of academic and professional research projects in international accounting and has experience in auditing multinational companies.

INTERNATIONAL AUDITING

A comparative survey of professional requirements in Australia, Canada, France, West Germany, Japan, the Netherlands, the UK and the USA

Leslie G. Campbell

St. Martin's Press   New York

Printed in Hong Kong
Published in the United Kingdom by The Macmillan Press Ltd
First published in the United States of America in 1985

ISBN 0-312-41969-4

Library of Congress Cataloging in Publication Data

Campbell, Leslie G., 1955–
  International auditing.

  Bibliography: p.
  Includes index.
  1. Auditing—Standards—Case studies.   I. Title.
HF5667. C257   1984   657′.45′0218   84–11643
ISBN 0-312-41969-4

To Jane

Contents

Foreword

During recent decades there have been many changes in the operations, financing and structure of businesses which operate across national frontiers (or 'multinational corporations' for short) and there is now a considerable literature dealing with various aspects of multinational business. A well-cultivated patch of this literature deals specifically with international aspects of accounting and financial reporting.

Until now there has been surprisingly little discussion about the auditing implications of international financial control and reporting. Leslie Campbell's book is therefore welcome as an extensive, imaginative and authoritative review of the issues involved. It constitutes an important contribution to the relevant literature for international auditors – practitioners and academics.

Recent developments within the accountancy profession have been marked by broad public interest in matters to do with accountancy measurement and financial reporting. The extent to which professional developments in these areas have implications for public policy has brought accountancy into the political arena (using the word 'political' in its broadest sense). In the United Kingdom, for example, the extent of this public interest is reflected in the work of the Accounting Standards Committee; the participation in the work of that Committee of non-accountants; the interest of trade-union organisations in information for employees; the impact on Company Law of Directives of the Commission of the European Communities; the continuing debate about 'inflation accounting'; the significance for financial reporting of the changes in fiscal arrangements introduced by the 1984 Budget. In all these and other related areas, accountants now have to recognise the political implications of their professional work. For those dealing with multinationals, the issues become even more complex at the transnational political level where, for example, organisations such as the OECD and the United Nations have become actively involved.

That part of the accountancy profession's concerns which is to do with auditing appears not to have such potentially sensitive political implications. Looking at the point in a parochial UK context, one can perhaps attempt to define the audit function as the expression of an independent opinion by an expert in financial reporting confirming (or not!) compliance with all relevant reporting requirements. The actual specification of these reporting requirements – usually embodied directly or indirectly in some legal code – will reflect broad public policy conclusions about appropriate financial measurement and disclosure, conclusions informed by professional accountancy advice. The expression of the audit opinion, however, still seems to be largely accepted as the quasi-judicial exercise of professional opinion. The definition of appropriate techniques of gathering and assessing evidence on which the audit opinion rests is broadly accepted as a primarily professional responsibility, and the public at large appears to have no particular desire to engage in debate about these professional processes. Of course, the community at large demands reassurance that recompense can be obtained by those who suffer loss due to the exercise of faulty professional judgement, and insists on the existence of processes by which the professional auditor can be called to account. This, of course, is ultimately through the Courts, but also includes the self-disciplinary measures by which the profession regulates the practitioner.

The point is very clearly made in a UK context when one contrasts the nature and extent of public comment on statements by the Accounting Standards Committee with that stimulated by the Auditing Practices Committee. Internationally, the work of the IASC has always aroused more comment and public interest than has the work of the Audit Practices Committee of the IFAC. Neither the OECD nor the UN has concerned itself with auditing the accounts of transnational corporations, but both have dealt extensively with accounting disclosure.

Multinational business has been changing and becoming relatively more significant both to the economies of their home territories as well as to those of the host nations to which their activities extend. There has developed in parallel the creation of large multinational groupings of audit firms. The audit firms have sought to ensure that both the shareholders and managements of their multinational clients could be assured of consistency of audit approach and consistency of quality of detailed audit work regardless of where the corporation's operations were conducted. The need to achieve quality control on an international basis strengthened previous relationships between the audit firm serving the multinational's headquarters and its correspondent audit firms elsewhere. These correspondent relationships coalesced into groupings of national or regional firms using one common name worldwide, sharing technical expertise and adopting common techniques as well as common philosophies and practices of exercising audit judgement.

The international audit firms thereby created networks of offices and personnel who were knowledgeable about accountancy and related financial management matters of all the territories in which any one multinational client was headquartered and operated. The audit firm could thus match the knowledge of different environments which its client's executive team could muster. In this way the audit firm became as sensitive to differences between different territories as did executives of its client. Auditors came to understand as well as did the management of multinational corporations that there are significant cultural differences among countries and these, in turn, influence economic activity and its related financial reporting within any one community.

There are parts of the world where the Anglo-Saxon view of auditing (expressed above) is not fully understood. In many countries auditing is seen primarily as a means of ensuring compliance with specified detailed reporting re- quirements. The expectation of the extent as well as the nature of the examination of records and the accumu- lation of other information as a basis for the audit opinion or certificate differs very dramatically from country to country.

These and other important issues receive attention from Mr Campbell. In every part of his text he makes an important contribution to the literature of his profession. His comparative analysis of auditing standards in the major countries in which multinational corporations are headquar- tered constitutes a firm foundation upon which he builds progressively. He rightly points up the importance of cultural influences and the difficulties of 'exporting' audit concepts from one community to another – even within what we like to call the 'developed western world'. His discussion of specific issues which arise in the audit of multinational corporations is informative as well as imaginative, and his views on the issues of harmonisation of auditing standards thought-provoking.

It is very gratifying that the recently established post- graduate degree of Master of Accountancy at the University of Glasgow should have flowered already in this important book by one of the first graduates from the course. I would rejoice in Mr Campbell's achievement for that reason alone, but do so all the more because of our joint involvement in

the work of Deloitte Haskins & Sells and, finally, because
we are both members of The Institute of Chartered
Accountants of Scotland.

J. C. Shaw

*President, The Institute of Chartered Accountants of Scotland
1983–4
Formerly, Johnstone Smith Professor of Accountancy, University of Glasgow, 1977–82*

Preface

This book is designed to bridge the gap that I believe exists between the literature on international financial reporting and the literature on auditing. It examines a number of international financial reporting issues from an auditing perspective, and it examines a number of auditing issues from an international perspective.

The book is both theoretical and practical. The theoretical aspects are found in the examination of issues referred to above, and the practical aspects are found in the detailed studies of auditing standards in eight developed countries.

The book is designed to appeal to academics and to practitioners. It can be used as part of undergraduate and graduate courses in international accounting or in auditing. The book should be useful to practitioners involved in the audit of multinational companies, and the chapters on comparative international auditing should prove useful to users of international financial statements. The international nature of the contents should appeal to readers around the world. In essence, the book should be of interest to anyone involved in auditing or in international financial reporting.

I am indebted to a number of people for their help and encouragement in writing this book. A great deal of useful information and comments were provided by Greg Pound of the Australian Accounting Research Foundation, Bob Ellis of the Institute of Chartered Accountants in Australia, David Selley of the Canadian Institute of Chartered

Accountants, Patrice Cardon of the *Ordre des Experts Comptables et des Comptables Agréés,* Peter Marks of the *Institut der Wirtschaftsprüfer,* T. Okubo of the Japanese Institute of Certified Public Accountants and Otto Volgenant of the *Nederlands Instituut van Registeraccountants.* A number of other professional sources supplied me with a wealth of material that will have to wait for another book. In this respect I would like to thank in particular Dr Rag. A. Castagnoli of the *Consiglio Nazionale dei Ragionieri e Periti Commerciali,* Paul Phenix of the Malaysian Association of Certified Public Accountants, Phil Gott of the South African Institute of Chartered Accountants and Mario Fernández of the *Instituto de Censores Jurados de Cuentas de España.*

Gijs Bak (chairman of the International Auditing Practices Committee of the International Federation of Accountants) and Matthew Patient (UK National Technical Partner of Deloitte Haskins & Sells) reviewed earlier drafts of this book and provided useful insights into national and international auditing environments. Graham McGregor and Ken Ueba (of Deloitte Haskins & Sells, Calgary and Tokyo respectively) also provided useful ideas and comments. Wayne Williamson and Ted Bluey (of Deloitte Haskins & Sells, New York and Washington DC respectively) made a number of helpful suggestions and critical comments.

In particular, I would like to thank Jack Shaw for writing the Foreword and for being living proof that the terms 'academic' and 'practitioner' are not mutually exclusive. I would also like to thank Professor Sidney Gray of the University of Glasgow for providing initial encouragement and advice. I am also grateful for the good nature and typing skills of Rosa Cahill, Rebecca Devitt and Heidi Yarwood.

Finally I would like to record my thanks to my wife Jane, who has been a constant source of help and encouragement. Like all good doctors, she rarely lost her patience.

Any errors or omissions are of course entirely my responsibility. All that remains to be said is that I hope that reading the book is as informative as writing it has been.

L.G.C.
London, February 1984

List of abbreviations

AA	Arthur Andersen
AAA	American Accounting Association
AARF	Australian Accounting Research Foundation
ACA	Association of Certified Accountants
AFDA	*Association Française pour le Developpement de l'Audit*
AICPA	American Institute of Certified Public Accountants
APC	Auditing Practices Committee
ASB	Auditing Standards Board
ASC	Accounting Standards Committee
AY	Arthur Young
BADC	Business Accounting Deliberation Council
BDO	Binder Dijker Otte
CCAB	Consultative Committee of Accountancy Bodies
CICA	Canadian Institute of Chartered Accountants
CIPFA	Chartered Institute of Public Finance and Accountancy
C&L	Coopers and Lybrand
CNC	*Conseil Nationale de la Comptabilité*
CNCC	*Compagnie Nationale des Commissaires aux Comptes*
COB	*Commission des Opérations de Bourse*
CPA	Certified Public Accountant
DH&S	Deloitte Haskins & Sells
EEC	European Economic Community
E&W	Ernst & Whinney

FASB	Financial Accounting Standards Board
FMI	Fox Moore International
GoB	*Grundsätzen ordnungsmässiger Buchführung* (proper accounting principles)
GTI	Grant Thornton International
HHI	Horwath and Horwath International
IAPC	International Auditing Practices Committee
IASC	International Accounting Standards Committee
ICAEW	Institute of Chartered Accountants in England and Wales
ICAI	Institute of Chartered Accountants in Ireland
ICAS	Institute of Chartered Accountants of Scotland
ICMA	Institute of Cost and Management Accountants
IdW	*Institut der Wirtschaftsprüfer in Deutschland e.V*
IFAC	International Federation of Accountants
JICPA	Japanese Institute of Certified Public Accountants
KMG	Klynveld Main Goerdeler
MNC	Multinational company
NFI	Non-Financial Information
NIVRA	*Nederlands Instituut van Registeraccountants*
OECCA	*Ordre des Experts Comptables et des Comptables Agréés*
OECD	Organisation for Economic Co-operation and Development
PMM	Peat Marwick Mitchell
PW	Price Waterhouse
SAS	Statement on Auditing Standards
SEC	Securities and Exchange Commission
Section 161 bodies	ICAEW, ICAI, ICAS, ACA
SGV	SyCip Gorres Velayo
SSAP	Statement of Standard Accounting Practice
TASC	Tripartite Accounting Standards Committee
TR	Touche Ross

UEC	*Union Européenne des Experts Comptables Economiques et Financiers*
UN	United Nations
WP	*Wirtschaftsprüfer*

Part 1
Introduction

1 Introduction

1.1 THE IMPORTANCE OF THE TOPIC

Issues in international auditing arise from two sources, namely the audit of multinational companies (MNCs) and the audit of non-domestic companies. The importance of international auditing is established below by considering each source in turn. The distinction between the two sources arises from the difference between foreign direct investment and foreign portfolio investment. In the case of foreign direct investment a company sets up branches or subsidiaries in other countries, and the company is usually described as a multinational where these foreign operations form a material part of the group's total activities. In the case of foreign portfolio investment a company or an individual buys shares in foreign companies, usually through the medium of foreign stock exchanges, although in some cases the foreign company may be listed on the domestic stock exchange. The distinction between direct and portfolio investment depends on the degree of control which can be exercised by the investor.

1.1.1 The Audit of MNCs

There may seem to be little need to expand on the importance of MNCs in the context of the international business scene. There is a wide range of literature on the subject of MNCs (for a useful introduction see Hood and

Young, 1979; Eiteman and Stonehill, 1982; or Dunning, 1974), and this reflects the significance of their impact both on their parent country and on the host countries in which their branches and subsidiaries operate. Home country impact can be measured in terms of the effect on national economic performance. For example, in the UK a substantial majority of the top 100 companies in *The Times 1000* (1983) can be considered to be MNCs. Consequently, MNCs have an important role to play in carrying out the country's economic and industrial policies. As well as this indirect effect on the individual's economic welfare, there may also be a direct effect on the individual as employee or as shareholder (either through direct shareholdings or via pension funds and insurance companies).

Benefits to the host country include the employment effects (in terms of new jobs and increased levels of training, both of which should have 'spillover' effects on the rest of the economy), assistance in industrialising the primarily agricultural economies of developing host countries, and the favourable impact on the host country's balance of payments and currency reserves of the subsidiary's exports from the host country. However, MNCs have on occasion been criticised from the host country viewpoint for importing technology rather than establishing a local research and development function, for importing senior management instead of training local management, and for disinvesting when it suits the MNC despite adverse consequences to the host country.

The size and nature of the MNCs gives them an extremely powerful position in the international business world, and justifies the study of MNCs and their operations. The relevance of the *audit* of MNCs is that the audit is an important means of ensuring that the MNC remains accountable to its shareholders. The separation of ownership and management which exists in nearly all MNCs means that a conflict of interest may arise beween those who own and those who manage the MNC. The owners may thus have reason to suspect the validity of the information contained in the MNC's annual corporate report, and therefore create a demand for the information to be examined and reported on by independent third parties – the auditors. The complexity of the MNC's operations and the difficulties in accessing the relevant information make it unlikely that an individual shareholder will feel confident in his ability to confirm the validity of the information himself, and this increases the demand for an external audit. Finally, the size of the MNCs means that the consequence of the decisions taken regarding MNCs tends to be of greater than usual significance, and so again there is a need to confirm the validity of the information on which these decisions are based.

The MNC audit is thus necessary in order to ensure the continuing accountability of the MNC to its shareholders. Other interested parties may also demand that the MNC should be accountable for the consequences of its actions, such as the consequences on its employees, or on society as a whole through the MNC's impact on government policies and objectives. From the auditor's viewpoint, the size and nature of MNCs means that although the MNC audit is prestigious and financially rewarding, it is also particularly complex and challenging, in that it raises several problems in addition to those involved in the audit of a large uninational company.

1.1.2 The Audit of Non-domestic Companies

The second source of issues in international auditing arises from the audit of non-domestic companies. The importance of these issues becomes apparent if viewed from the perspective of a user of non-domestic financial statements. In addition to facing potential differences in generally accepted accounting principles, the user of non-domestic financial statements also faces potential differences in generally accepted auditing standards. When the user is determining the reliance he can place on the financial statements, a crucial factor is the amount of credibility added by the audit report. In order to assess the extent of this 'added credibility' (discussed further in Chapter 2), the user must understand the nature and purpose of the foreign audit. Consequently, an appreciation of the issues in comparative international auditing seems essential for the user of non-domestic financial statements.

Another useful perspective to adopt is that of the body responsible for issuing auditing standards. This may be a government agency or the national accounting profession, and it may be issuing codified auditing standards for the first time or amending the existing standards. Whatever the exact situation, the standard-setting body could benefit from knowing how similar bodies in other countries have approached the problem. This requires an understanding of the differences and the similarities in the audit environments, and again calls for an appreciation of the issues in comparative international auditing.

International auditing is therefore of importance to anyone interested in international financial reporting, used in its widest sense to include the financial reports of multinationals and of foreign companies. As international trade and international investment increase, so too does the significance of international financial reporting and hence of international auditing.

1.2 THE STRUCTURE OF THE BOOK

This book is divided into four parts. Part I includes this introductory chapter and also a chapter that analyses the need for auditing and for auditing standards. That analysis provides a background to the issues that are discussed later in the book. Part II deals with comparative international auditing, and consists of short chapters that examine the auditing standards and the financial reporting environments in eight countries, namely Australia, Canada, France, Germany, Japan, the Netherlands, the United Kingdom and the United States. These countries were selected on the basis of their economic significance and/or the developed nature of their accounting professions. Part III considers a number of other issues in international auditing. The first two chapters in Part III analyse the issues that arise in the audit of an MNC. The next chapter considers the harmonisation issue. International harmonisation of auditing standards may be a solution to the problems discussed in the preceding two chapters. Harmonisation may also be a solution to the problems that confront an international user of financial statements who is faced with the differences outlined in Part II. The subsequent chapter concerns the audit implications of the disclosure by MNCs of non-financial information. The final chapter in Part III analyses the structures and strategies of the international auditing firms. Part IV provides a summary and suggests areas for further research.

2 The Need for Auditing Standards

2.1 INTRODUCTION

One of the recurring themes in this book is the topic of auditing standards in an international context. Chapters 3 to 10 deal with comparative international auditing standards, Chapter 11 analyses the issues involved in transferring domestic auditing standards overseas and Chapter 13 discusses the international harmonisation of auditing standards. This chapter provides some background to these later chapters by examining the rationale underlying the existence of auditing standards. An understanding of why auditing standards exist seems to be a necessary pre-condition of appreciating international differences and similarities in auditing standards and appreciating the issues raised in applying auditing standards to MNC audits. Raising the question 'Why auditing standards?' leads to a more fundamental question, namely 'Why audit?'. This is the basic question that must be addressed in any discussion relating to auditing.

Section 2.2 outlines the arguments put forward to justify the need for auditing. It includes a discussion of how these arguments can be considered to be of particular relevance to the audit of MNCs. It also reviews some recent research into stock market reactions to qualified audit reports, and assesses the extent to which this research can be interpreted as measuring the value of auditing. Section 2.3 outlines the arguments put forward to justify the need for auditing standards. It deals separately with the need for abstract

auditing standards and the need for codified auditing
standards. It also includes a discussion of how those
arguments can be considered to be of particular relevance to
the audit of MNCs.

2.2   WHY AUDIT?

2.2.1   **The Lending of Credibility**

The superficial answer to the 'Why audit?' question in the
UK context is that an audit is necessary because it is a legal
requirement. The source of this legal requirement is section
14(1) of the Companies Act 1967, as amended by Schedule 2
of the Companies Act 1976. This states that

> The auditors of a company shall make a report to the
> members on the accounts examined by them, and on
> every balance sheet, every profit and loss account and all
> group accounts prepared under section 1 of the Com-
> panies Act 1976 (or under that section taken with section
> 150 of the principal Act), of which, in accordance with
> section 1(6) of the said Act of 1976, a copy is laid before
> the company in general meeting during their tenure of
> office.

However, this legal requirement is only the codification of a
deeper underlying need for the audit function. This is often
considered to be the need for the lending of credibility to the
company's financial statements. Stamp and Moonitz (1978)
say that 'the function of auditing is to lend credibility to
financial statements'. Mautz (1975) says that 'Stated simply
auditing adds credibility to financial statements.' Shaw
(1980) states that 'The audit opinion lends credibility to the
directors' financial reporting . . .' The ultimate impact of the
'added credibility' on the process of resource allocation is

recognised by Anderson (1977), who says that the role of auditing is to add credibility to financial statements and thus to enhance the effectiveness of accounting communication needed by the economic system.

The 'lending of credibility' argument is based on the premise that financial statements will be of more use to the various user groups if the financial statements have been examined and reported on by independent auditors. This added usefulness is derived from the reduction in the risk to the user groups that the financial statements may include materially distorted information. The conclusion of this argument is therefore that the audit function improves the quality of the information provided to the user groups. The American Accounting Association research study (1973) summarises this argument by saying that the user of accounting information must make two types of judgement. Firstly, he must interpret the *content* of the information, and secondly he must evaluate the *quality* of the information. The research study states that the function of auditing is to assist the user in making this second judgement.

2.2.2 The Accountability Argument

Another perspective on the need for auditing is given by the accountability argument. The concept of accountability can be considered on two levels, namely the narrow legal concept and the wider social concept (Shaw, 1980). The narrow legal concept recognises that the owners of the business have entrusted certain resources to the directors. This raises the need for the directors to report to the owners on how the directors have used these resources. The owners of the business can then use this information to assess whether the directors have made proper use of the resources under their control. The precise definition of 'proper use' will depend on the objectives of the owners of the business.

Jack (1983) points out that the concept of accountability may produce a conflict in the duties of the directors. On the one hand, the fiduciary aspect of accountability dictates that the directors are responsible for the stewardship of the resources entrusted to them. Consequently, the directors are in the position of trustees. On the other hand, the owners of the business will assess the directors on the basis of their performance, and this need for profitability involves an element of risk-taking which is inconsistent with their position as trustees. These conflicting aspects of accountability lead to demands for different types of information to be given to the owners of the business. The wider social concept of accountability recognises that shareholders are not the only group in society affected by the actions of the directors. There are other interested parties who claim a right to be given information on how the directors' actions impinge on them. This wider social concept of accountability is dealt with in more detail in Chapter 14, which also discusses the auditing implications.

Therefore the accountability argument establishes the need for the provision of certain information by the directors of the business to its owners. The need for auditing is explained by introducing the monitoring concept, which says that the information provided by the directors must be suitably monitored by a third party (that is, the auditor). The third party is responsible for expressing an opinion on the information conveyed by the directors. The shareholders are then better placed to assess whether the directors have fulfilled their obligations. The monitoring aspect of the accountability argument is summarised by Flint (1982), who says that an audit is a monitoring process comparing conduct or performance with the social norms that have been established to define the particular duty of accountability. The reference to 'social norms' is a useful reminder that the nature of accountability differs over time and between countries in response to the particular cultural and business environment. This point is also made by Tricker (1980), who says that the practice of auditing develops in response to changing demands for accountability in society. Tricker argues that demands for accountability change in response to specific corporate collapses or crises, and consequently that changes in the audit function are the result, not the cause, of changes in social expectations of accountability. Tricker supports this argument by providing a brief history of the development of the demands for corporate accountability in the UK and the US over the last 150 years.

2.2.3 Conflict of Interests, Consequence, Complexity and Remoteness

The similarities and the shortcomings of the added credibility argument and the accountability argument can be highlighted by considering the 'Why audit?' question from the perspective adopted in the American Accounting Association research study (1973). This takes the analysis a stage further by explaining why a potential credibility gap exists (and consequently why there is a need to 'add credibility'). It also synthesises the concepts of accountability and monitoring into a single theoretical framework. The AAA research study argues that the demand for auditing arises from four factors, namely conflict of interest, consequence, complexity and remoteness.

Conflict of interest may arise when the objectives of the user of financial statements differ from the objectives of the preparer. When these objectives differ, the user may be concerned about possible bias in the information presented to him. These doubts about the quality of the information create the need for an independent third party to assess the quality of this information. As the AAA research study says, this assessment may in certain cases be performed directly by the user himself, but due to reasons of complexity and remoteness it is unlikely that the user will be able to perform this assessment adequately.

'Consequence' refers to the importance to the user of the decisions taken by him on the basis of the financial statements. This factor recognises that the process of communication from the preparer to the user of financial statements will normally result in providing information which will help the user in making decisions. The more important these decisions are, the more concerned the user will be about the reliability of the information he is being given. The implicit argument is that an independent audit is the best way of attaining assurance as to this reliability.

The complexity factor is explained as follows: as economic reality and the accounting systems for recording that reality become more complex, the user faces increasing difficulties in satisfying himself directly that the financial statements are a proper distillation of the underlying economic events. In addition, this greater complexity increases the chances of errors arising in the measurement and reporting process. This creates a need for someone with sufficient technical proficiency to cope with this complexity and report back to the users.

The remoteness factor arises from the separation of ownership and control of the business, and also from the separation of the user from the subject matter of the information he receives. This remoteness results in the user being unable to verify the financial statement information directly. Direct verification by the user may be impossible due to physical remoteness, legal or institutional barriers, or simply lack of time and money to perform an adequate investigation himself. Financial statements users may therefore consider that it makes sense to delegate the verification process to someone who can surmount these remoteness difficulties. Such delegation also removes the need for multiple investigations (that is, one by each user).

The AAA research study considers that as these four

factors increase in intensity, they interact in such a way as to make it not only more important that the user properly evaluates the quality of the information he receives, but also more difficult for the user to perform such an evaluation without the assistance of a third party. The research study concludes that the four factors combine to create a demand for the satisfaction of the attest function by an independent third party.

2.2.4 Socio-political Views of Corporate Regulation

Another view on the role of auditing is provided by Tricker (1980) who argues that auditing must be considered in its socio-political context rather than being examined from any single perspective. Tricker argues that auditing is part of the system of controls that modern society has created to regulate the powers of the corporate sector. Companies themselves (or more accurately, their directors and managers) are seen as willing participants in this system, because they are considered to accept the regulatory network as being the price they have to pay in return for the right of control over the stakeholders' interests. The stakeholders include not only the shareholders but also other interested parties such as lenders, creditors, employees and the general public. Influences on the regulatory system include company law and the courts, government agencies and departments, self-regulatory bodies and professional associations.

This socio-political argument is therefore an extension of the accountability argument discussed earlier. Tricker admits that this aspect of the accountability argument has still to be developed in detail, and he argues that there is a need for a proper theory of corporate accountability.

2.2.5 Agency Theory

A different perspective on the demand for auditing is

provided by agency theory. This is discussed in Jensen and Meckling (1976) and in Benston (1979/80). The common thread running through the theories described earlier in this chapter is that they all explain why the *user* of financial information perceives a need for that information to be audited. One of the underlying premises of these theories is that management is likely to introduce a bias into the financial information it prepares for external use. Agency theory suggests however that *preparers* of financial information perceive a need for that information to be audited. As Chow and Rice (1982a) say, the exponents of this theory argue that the manager can benefit from letting shareholders monitor his allocation of the firm's resources. The theory says that a company's directors will approve of the audit function, as they consider that the audit improves the credibility of their financial reporting. This improved credibility is likely to improve the directors' status, salaries and share valuations compared to a situation where there is no audit and a higher level of uncertainty concerning the financial position and performance of the company. Agency theory suggests that the directors consider that these benefits outweigh the costs of auditing. From the directors' viewpoint, the costs of auditing include the audit fee and the costs of managerial and employee time spent dealing with the auditors. The costs of auditing also include the 'cost' to the directors of being discouraged from introducing bias into the financial information. Skerratt (1982) summarises the arguments of agency theory by saying that an audit increases the value of the information disclosed by the company. For a given level of disclosed earnings the value of the company will increase, and this benefits the manager.

2.2.6 Empirical Research

Some researchers have attempted to see whether the need

for auditing can be proved or disproved by empirical research. This research has examined the reaction of stock markets to qualified audit reports and has also conducted 'laboratory' tests to determine user group reactions to qualified reports. The various studies do not provide conclusive proof of the value of the audit function, but in general they support the conclusion that the audit report is valued by the users of financial information.

Estes and Reimer (1977) provided audit reports, financial statements and background information to a specific user group, namely bankers, to test whether qualified audit reports had any effect on their decision to advance loans. A test group of bankers was provided with the basic financial information plus an audit report containing an 'except for' qualification. A control group was given the same basic financial information plus a standard unqualified audit report. The difference between the subsequent financial decision-making of the two groups was not statistically significant, and hence the evidence could not support the conclusion that an 'except for' audit opinion would damage the company's prospects of a loan being advanced. This could be interpreted as implying that there is no added value to be gained from the audit function.

Estes and Reimer (1979) repeated this test on a different user group, namely financial analysts. In this case, the research was designed to test whether the share price estimates of the analysts would be affected by an 'except for' opinion. This time the difference between the control group and the test group *was* statistically significant. Estes and Reimer concluded that the evidence supported the conclusion that an 'except for' opinion has a negative effect on share evaluations by financial analysts.

Firth (1978) studied the effects of certain types of audit qualifications on share prices of UK companies. The methodology used was to compare the actual security returns against those expected had there been no qualification. This 'expected' return was given by the market model, which measured the returns for a particular security against that of the average returns for the market as a whole. Firth's results showed that investors reacted adversely (by significantly reducing share prices) in the case of three particular types of audit qualifications, namely those relating to the general 'true and fair view', going concern and asset values. Firth concluded that certain types of qualified audit reports contain significant information that investors use in their portfolio decision-making.

Ball, Walker and Whittred (1979) studied a sample of Australian companies' audit qualifications. They (like Firth) examined share price movements around the date of the announcement of the audit report, and compared these movements with the market model. They too sub-divided their sample into certain types of qualification. Their results showed that qualifications relating to non-depreciation of buildings were associated with increases in share prices. This seems surprising as such qualifications would indicate that actual net profit is less than the reported net profit. Their results also showed that (contrary to their hypothesis) qualifications as to asset valuations were not associated with significant share price decreases. There was some evidence that the remaining group of 'other qualifications' were associated with share price reductions. The results of this study are interesting but seem to be less conclusive than those of Firth.

Chow and Rice (1982b) noted the limitations of Firth and of Ball *et al.*, and also warned against generalising from the UK or Australian environment to the US one. Chow and Rice examined the share price movements of a sample of US firms with qualified audit reports (the treatment sample). These share price movements were compared with those of a control sample of US firms with unqualified audit reports. The two samples were matched by sales, by industry classification and by auditor. The samples were also considered to have reasonably similar systematic risk. One of the research objectives was to focus on firm-specific stock returns, and consequently a model was designed in such a way as to control for market and industry-wide influences. The results showed a statistically significant difference between the returns of the treatment sample and the control sample. Chow and Rice conclude that this is consistent with the hypothesis that qualified audit reports have negative impacts on share prices. Their evidence also suggests that different types of qualifications have different effects on share prices. In particular, 'asset realisation' qualifications have a relatively larger negative impact than 'uncertainty' qualifications. Chow and Rice add the caveat that the negative correlation between qualified opinions and price changes does not necessarily imply a causal relationship.

The above paragraphs provide a brief summary of some empirical research into the role of the audit function. In general, the research supports the hypothesis that the audit report is valued by particular user groups. However, some of the conclusions appear to be contradictory, and most of the studies admit to the methodological limitations of the research performed to date. Perhaps all that can be said with certainty is that the studies demonstrate the difficulty of applying empirical research to the 'Why audit?' question.

2.2.7 The Particular Relevance to MNCs

This section places the preceding discussion in an international context by demonstrating why there is a particular need for the audit of MNCs. This is demonstrated by applying the theoretical arguments specifically to the case of MNCs. The 'lending of credibility' argument and the accountability argument are effectively sub-components of the arguments in the AAA research study (1973) discussed in 2.2.3 above, and consequently the discussion in this section concentrates on the four factors suggested by that research study.

There are likely to be more conflicts of interest between the user and preparer of MNC financial statements than of non-MNC financial statements. This is partly for reasons of size, in that MNCs tend to be relatively large and consequently their financial statements could be expected to have a higher number of users. There might therefore be a wider range of objectives among users, compared with the non-MNC case, and this would increase the likelihood of differences in objectives between users and preparers of financial statements. In addition, the mix of users is likely to be more varied in the case of MNCs, in that the users would tend to come from a broader range of national backgrounds than in the case of non-MNCs. These different national environments may lead to a greater range of user objectives (for example, bankers in France may have different objectives, and different lending criteria, compared with their UK counterparts). This would again increase the likelihood of differences in objectives between the user and preparer of financial statements.

The consequence argument is likely to be particularly applicable to MNCs. This is again due to their relative size, which would suggest that the information in MNC financial statements is likely to be used for decisions of relatively greater consequence.

The complexity argument also seems particularly relevant to MNCs. The international business environment includes several factors which create additional uncertainties and complexities for the MNC in comparison with the non-MNC. Among these factors are foreign currency exchange risk, differences in commercial environments, differences in national legal systems, possibilities of host government appropriation of company assets and comparative differences in attitudes and abilities of management and employees. The economic activities of the MNC in response to these factors are likely to be more complex than in the non-MNC case. The user of MNC financial statements is therefore faced with comprehending a more complex set of economic events, and consequently it seems that there is a particular need for someone with sufficient technical proficiency to cope with this complexity and report to the users.

The remoteness factor is also particularly relevant to MNCs, in that the user is likely to face even greater difficulties in gaining access to the accounting records and to the related economic events. Physical access will probably be more difficult in the case of MNCs, because of the international spread of operations, and in addition there may be particular legal or institutional barriers to access in certain countries.

The socio-political arguments for auditing can be emphasised in the case of MNCs, in that the need for the regulation of corporate behaviour is especially important in the case of companies with the greatest ability to exercise power. A popular view of MNCs is that they fall into this category. The particular relevance of agency theory to MNCs is that directors and senior management of MNCs are likely to have relatively higher status, salaries and related benefits, and consequently have relatively greater incentive to improve the credibility of their financial reporting by demanding an external audit.

2.3 WHY AUDITING STANDARDS?

The term 'auditing standards' refers to the basic principles which guide the conduct of the auditor. Auditing standards differ from auditing practices (or auditing procedures), which refer to the detailed ways in which the auditing standards are applied in practice. Picking (1973) explains the difference by saying that auditing standards remain the same from audit to audit while procedures change to suit the circumstances. Auditing standards are therefore on a higher, more conceptual level than auditing procedures. Stamp and Moonitz (1978) draw an analogy with the field of accounting, where accounting concepts (or accounting objectives) form the highest level of generalisation, and accounting standards (and accounting policies) are deduced from these high-level 'first principles'. As Stamp and Moonitz point out, this analogy brings out the difference between the word 'standards' in the auditing context and its use in the accounting context.

In this section a distinction is made between abstract auditing standards and codified auditing standards. Abstract auditing standards refer to certain generalised concepts relating to the auditor's professional qualities, whereas codified auditing standards refer to a specific set of these concepts agreed and published by professional accounting bodies (or by the government). The distinction is important because there are different reasons for the two types of auditing standards.

2.3.1 The Need for Abstract Auditing Standards

In this subsection 'auditing standards' refers to abstract auditing standards rather than to codified auditing standards, which are dealt with in the next subsection.

It has been argued that a set of auditing standards is a vital component in the structure of auditing as a field of knowledge. Mautz and Sharaf (1961) conclude their study by building a model of auditing knowledge. This starts with the philosophical foundations of auditing, out of which can be drawn the postulates of auditing. 'Postulates' refer to the assumptions used as a basis of inference in constructing a theoretical model. Auditing postulates include for example the assumption that financial statements and financial data are verifiable. From these postulates are developed the essential auditing concepts, which form the conceptual structure described by Mautz and Sharaf as the elemental generalisations around which the bulk of auditing theory is organised. These auditing concepts refer to what are now more commonly known as auditing standards. The concepts give rise to auditing 'precepts', which refer to the guidelines developed to show how the concepts should be applied. Finally, there are the practical applications of the precepts to actual situations. This brief explanation of the Mautz and Sharaf model shows the importance of auditing standards (or concepts) in developing a theory of auditing. Stamp and Moonitz (1978) reach a similar conclusion in stating that auditing standards occupy the highest level of generality in the hierarchy of ideas, concepts and prescriptions that constitute the intellectual structure of the auditing profession.

A different approach is found in the argument that auditing standards are a necessary condition for achieving public confidence in the audit opinion. In this case, the 'lending of credibility' argument is applied not to the effect of an audit on the financial statements, but to the effect of auditing standards on the audit opinion (Stamp and Moonitz, 1978). Flint (1980) considers that the perceived auditing standards are vital for establishing the confidence of the users of audit opinions. This approach to the need for auditing standards could be summarised as follows: the basic premise is that society has entrusted the auditing profession with the responsibility of monitoring corporate accountability, and the argument is that this monitoring function could be removed from the hands of the auditing profession if society considers that audit quality is falling short of some ideal level of auditing standards.

The need for *particular* auditing standards (as opposed to the need for a general *set* of auditing standards) can be traced directly from the reasons behind the need for auditing as discussed in Section 2.2. In particular, the model in the

AAA research study (1973) could be elaborated on as follows: if we accept that the *conflict of interests* between the preparers and users of financial statements gives rise to the need for an audit, then it seems logical to suggest that the auditor's interests should be sufficiently different from those of the preparers, so that he can express an impartial opinion on the financial statements. The argument can be extended to say that the auditor's interests should not be too closely identified with any one particular user group (or sub-group), in case the auditor's opinion is influenced by the effect his report might have on himself as a member of that particular group. This gives rise to the concept of auditor independence. The *consequence* reason for auditing arose from the importance to the user of the decisions he makes on the basis of the information provided in the financial statements. It could be argued that the consequence reason implies that the auditor must exercise due professional care in the performance of his audit. Such due professional care could include compliance with certain performance standards. The *complexity* of the information in the financial statements and of the underlying transactions means that the auditor must have an adequate level of education and training. Finally, the *remoteness* of the user from the accounting records and economic events implies that the auditor must be able to have access to the facts, figures and opinions used by the directors in preparing the financial statements. Taken together, the four reasons for auditing imply that the auditor must communicate the results of his audit to the users of the financial statements, thus giving rise to the need for standards of reporting. The above analysis can be used to demonstrate the need for standards of independence, due professional care, performance standards, competence (or education and training) and reporting. Similar conclusions (although not based on the AAA research study) were reached by Picking (1973), who attempted to deduce certain auditing standards from the basic proposition that whatever increases the reliance of the public in the audit opinion is a desirable feature or standard against which to judge the auditor. Picking concluded that this approach produced four categories of auditing standards, namely competence, independence, performance and reporting.

2.3.2 The Need for Codified Auditing Standards

The arguments in favour of having abstract auditing standards seem to be widely accepted. There is of course still much debate on exactly how these standards should be interpreted in particular circumstances. For example, there are differing views within the UK on how auditors should receive their education and training. However, there seems to be a general consensus that abstract auditing standards are a necessary part of the audit function.

The position of codified auditing standards is perhaps not so clearcut. Opponents of codification could point to the history of auditing developments in the UK, where for over a hundred years auditors practised their profession apparently unhindered by the lack of codified auditing standards. It could be argued that the conceptual nature of auditing standards requires the 'unwritten rules' approach, in that committing such standards to paper only creates problems of interpretation and does little to add to auditing as a field of knowledge. Furthermore, the courts are always available to any interested party who considers that an auditor has not properly fulfilled his duties. Such arguments conclude that the auditor's professional training should inculcate sufficiently rigorous *internalised* standards, and consequently there is no need for formal codification of these standards.

The above arguments (implicit or explicit) prevailed in the UK until the late 1970s. The codified auditing standards programme that developed around that time was seen by some commentators as being a direct consequence of public criticism of the auditing profession. Woolf (1979) asserts that the introduction of the UK Auditing Standards resulted from unprecedented public and government disapproval. Moir (1980) places the UK standards programme against a background of rapid change to the auditing environment. This change led to an increasing number of allegations of audit failures, and also to a 'veritable deluge' of Department of Trade Inspectors' reports, many of which referred to supposed audit deficiencies. Therefore one argument for the codification of auditing standards is that such codification makes it clear to the public that the profession does have auditing standards, against which performance in particular audits can be measured. An underlying motive from the profession's viewpoint may be that the development of codified auditing standards is one way of showing that the profession is capable of self-regulation, and consequently that government regulation is not necessary.

The above argument for codification is really part of a wider argument, namely that codification is needed (even in the absence of growing public and government concern) in order to educate the users of audit reports. It is argued that codification will help the users to understand the audit function more clearly. Gough (1978) says that although auditors know how they go about their work, the people who employ them do not, and the primary objective of the UK auditing standards programme is to remedy this defect. An editorial in *The Accountant's Magazine* (1980b) argued that the consequences of codification should include a lessening of the mystique surrounding the audit function and an increase in user comprehension of what the audit report means.

Another argument for codification is based on a 'producer' perspective rather than a user perspective. This argument states that although the individual auditor (rather than the profession) is ultimately responsible for determining his own standards of work, the individual auditor will nevertheless gain a significant benefit from having a set of professionally authorised standards against which he can measure his own performance. By examining this set of codified standards, the individual auditor can gain an understanding of how his profession perceives the standards expected by the various users of audit reports. A comparison of this perception against his own should help the individual to construct a framework within which to place his own beliefs as to the standards required. In addition, changes to the codified standards should help to inform the individual as to changes in social expectations of the audit function. This argument for codification is therefore essentially one of educating the preparers, not the users, of audit reports. Flint (1980) says that in codifying auditing standards the professional bodies are seeking to improve the quality of auditing practice by informing auditors of the standards of performance by which their own practice should be guided. Picking (1973) puts it more colloquially by saying that one of the reasons for the codification of auditing standards by the professional bodies is 'to keep members on their toes'.

Another aspect of the codification argument is that codification provides a benchmark against which a court of law may measure an auditor's performance. For example, paragraph 7 of the explanatory foreword of the UK Auditing Standards states that

> Members are advised that a court of law may, when considering the adequacy of the work of an auditor, take into account any pronouncements or publications which it thinks may be indicative of good practice. Auditing Standards and Guidelines are likely to be so regarded.

This implies that compliance with the codified standards is not an end in itself, but is a means to the end of fulfilling the duties imposed by law.

2.3.3   **The Particular Relevance to MNCs**

The above arguments for codified auditing standards seem
to be of particular relevance in the case of MNCs. In
general, the users of an MNC's financial statements will be
located in a wider range of countries than in the case of a
uninational company. An MNC audit report signed in
London may be examined by investors and analysts on the
New York stock exchange, by lenders in France and by
employees in Australia. These users may be unfamiliar with
auditing standards outside their own country, and consequently the information content of the audit report would
probably be relatively higher in cases where the users can
refer to a set of codified auditing standards which governed
the conduct of the audit. In such cases the user could assess
the value of the audit by comparing these auditing standards
with those in his own country (or with some other set of
auditing standards), and consequently could judge the
extent to which the audit does in fact lend credibility to the
financial statements.

It can be argued that codified auditing standards are also
of use to the auditors of the MNC's overseas subsidiaries,
particularly where these auditors are not familiar with the
auditing standards in the country of the MNC's parent
company. A set of codified auditing standards gives the
overseas auditors a brief summary of the standards against
which their performance may be measured.

Section 2.3.2 argued that the need for codified auditing
standards arose from the need to educate users and
producers of the audit report. Section 2.3.3 can be summarised by saying that this need for education is particularly
important in the international context.

2.4   SUMMARY

This chapter has discussed some of the fundamental issues

concerning the need for auditing and the need for auditing standards. The arguments were placed in an international context by assessing their particular relevance to MNCs. The matters discussed in this chapter provide an important foundation for the theoretical and practical issues in the chapters which follow.

Part II
Comparative International Auditing

3 Australia

3.1 THE AUDITING AND ACCOUNTING ENVIRONMENT

The dominant influences on the Australian accounting environment arise from legal and professional sources. Australian company law was originally modelled very closely on UK company law (Standish, 1981). However, the underlying political economy developed in such a way as to resemble the US system more than the UK system. An important example of this is the federal nature of the constitution, resulting in the various state parliaments each enacting their own Companies Acts. In practice this distinction was of little relevance, as the principal Act (until recently) was the Companies Act 1961, whose form and content was agreed by all the states before enactment in their individual jurisdictions. However, some subsequent amendments to this Act were passed in some states but not in others. An important change to the legislative procedure has occurred over the last few years with the introduction of a more standardised approach to company law. This new approach is based on a formal agreement beween the national government and the state governments (Parker, 1982), and has resulted in the National Companies Act 1981. One of the important features of the agreement is the creation of the National Companies and Securities Commission (NCSC), which is responsible for company administration and the regulation of the securities markets. The NCSC has already made an impact on the financial reporting

33

environment by issuing an exposure draft that proposes significant changes to the disclosure requirements affecting Australian companies *(International Accounting Bulletin,* 1983a). The legal influence on the auditing environment stems from the requirement for all companies to appoint an auditor (Johnston *et al.,* 1979). There are, however, certain exceptions for exempt proprietary companies (normally small family businesses), provided all the members of the company agree that an auditor is not necessary and this fact is duly minuted.

The professional influence on the Australian accounting environment arises from a well-developed accounting profession, represented by the members of the two professional bodies, namely the Institute of Chartered Accountants in Australia and the Australian Society of Accountants. The accounting profession has traditionally played an important role in establishing standards of financial reporting, as the government seemed to be content to set out a broad legislative framework within which the profession could lay down more detailed rules. However, the recent introduction of the NCSC seems to indicate that government influences on financial reporting are likely to predominate in the near future. The professional standard-setting process is carried out by the Australian Accounting Research Foundation (AARF), which is sponsored by the two professional bodies.

3.2 AUDITING STANDARDS – SOURCE, HISTORY AND AUTHORITY

A codified set of auditing standards has existed in Australia since 1951. The current auditing standards are found in Statement AUS, 'Statement of Auditing Standards and Statements of Auditing Practice', and Statement AUS 1, 'Statement of Auditing Standards'. Statement AUS provides brief background details to the auditing standards programme, whereas AUS 1 consists of the actual standards themselves. The standards are supported by a series of Statements of Auditing Practice (AUPs), which provide authoritative guidance as to how the standards may be applied.

The standards are prepared by the Auditing Standards Board (ASB) of the AARF, but are issued jointly by the Institute of Chartered Accountants in Australia and the Australian Society of Accountants. The AUPs are now prepared by the ASB and issued directly by the AARF. Some of the early AUPs in the current series were prepared by the Australian Audit Standards Committee, one of the technical committees of the AARF. The ASB was formed in 1981, and consists of nine members, being four from each of the professional bodies plus (as an ex-officio member) the Australian representative on the International Auditing Practices Committee (IAPC) of the International Federation of Accountants (IFAC). Although the ASB members are all professional accountants, they do not all come from private sector auditing firms. The variety of backgrounds is indicated in the ASB membership in December 1982, when five of the nine members were partners in firms of chartered accountants, two were finance directors of public companies, one was a state auditor-general and one was an internal auditor (Pound, 1982).

The first set of codified auditing standards was issued in 1951 under the heading of 'Statement on General Principles of Professional Auditing Practice'. This was revised and re-issued under the same title in 1954, 1969 and 1974, and was then revised and re-issued in 1977 as Statement AUS and Statement AUS 1 (referred to earlier). AUS and AUS 1 were subsequently revised and re-issued in 1983, following the ASB's decision to incorporate the IAPC's international auditing guidelines directly into the Australian standards. This decision also affects the Statements of Auditing Practice, and the most recent of these (AUP 9 to AUP 17) are based on the international auditing guidelines. Further evidence of the close relationship between the IAPC and the ASB is the ASB's decision to regard IAPC exposure drafts as being Australian auditing exposure drafts. It is argued that this will allow the Australian auditing profession to utilise the research efforts of IAPC and hence avoid unnecessary duplication of work at the national level. It is also argued that the Australian response to the international exposure draft will assist the ASB in the 'Australianisation' of IAPC guidelines. Although there is a close relationship between the IAPC and the ASB, members of the two Australian professional bodies are only expected to comply with the provisions of the Australian Statements. Paragraph 9 of Statement AUS says that it is the ASB's responsibility to ensure that compliance with the Australian Statements ensures compliance with international auditing guidelines. The ASB will include a note in any of the Australian Statements where statutory or other local conditions lead to incompatibility between the Australian Statements and the international auditing guidelines.

As far as the authority of the auditing standards is concerned, Statement AUS makes it clear that the standards set out in AUS 1 are mandatory. Statement AUS 1 repeats this term, and says that the standards state principles of audit conduct and performance that must be followed. Paragraph 4 of Statement AUS 1 describes the sanctions which apply in cases of non-compliance. Failure to observe the standards in Statement AUS 1 may result in investigation and disciplinary action. The Statements of Auditing Practice (the AUP series) are not mandatory, in that the practices set out may be varied to meet the requirements of particular audits. However, Statement AUS indicates that the AUPs provide authoritative guidance on the ways in which the auditing standards may be applied. Statement AUS also states that significant departures from the AUPs should be recorded in the working papers, and such a record should include both details of, and reasons for, the departure.

3.3 AUDITING STANDARDS – SCOPE AND CONTENT

The auditing standards in Statement AUS 1 apply to all audits. Paragraph 2 defines an audit as 'the independent examination of financial information of any entity, whether profit oriented or not, and irrespective of its size, or legal form, when such an examination is conducted with a view to expressing an opinion thereon'. There are therefore no limitations on the scope of the Australian auditing standards.

Statement AUS 1 is divided into two parts, namely 'Part I – Preface', and 'Part II – Auditing Standards'. Part I describes the scope and authority of the standards. It also describes the objective of an audit, which is stated as being to enable an auditor to express an opinion on the financial information. It indicates that this opinion helps to establish the credibility of the financial information, although it makes it clear that the entity's management is responsible for the actual preparation of the financial information. Part I also refers to the scope and the limitations of an audit. The scope is normally determined by reference to the relevant legislation and the terms of the audit engagement, as well as by reference to the Statements of Auditing Standards and Practice. The preface mentions the importance of judgement in the audit process, and emphasises that absolute certainty in auditing is rarely attainable. It also states that there is always a risk that some material misstatement may not be discovered.

Part II consists of the auditing standards themselves. The headings in Part II are as follows:

- Integrity, objectivity and independence

- Confidentiality
- Skills and competence
- Work performed by assistants
- Work performed by other auditors and experts
- Documentation
- Planning
- Audit evidence
- Accounting system and internal control
- Audit conclusions and reporting

The first three headings could be considered to represent general standards, the next six performance standards and the last one reporting standards. The paragraph on 'integrity, objectivity and independence' expands on each of these three terms. It says that the auditor should be straightforward, honest and sincere in his professional approach, and that the auditor must be fair, unprejudiced and unbiased. As far as independence is concerned, the standard says the auditor must have an impartial attitude and must not only be, but also appear to be, free of any interest which might be regarded as being incompatible with integrity and objectivity. The standard on 'confidentiality' states that the auditor should not disclose to a third party any information obtained in the course of his audit, unless he has been given specific authority to do so or unless there is a legal or professional duty to disclose. The 'skills and competence' standard requires that the audit should be carried out (and the report prepared) with due professional care by persons who have adequate training, experience and competence in auditing.

The standard on 'work performed by assistants' requires the careful direction, supervision and review by the auditor of any work delegated to assistants. The standard on 'work performed by other auditors and experts' emphasises that the auditor remains responsible for the audit opinion, even though he may have used the work performed by other auditors or experts. The auditor should therefore obtain reasonable assurance that such work is adequate for his purpose. The 'documentation' standard states that the auditor should record all matters which are important in providing evidence that the audit was carried out in accordance with the auditing standards and the practice statements. The 'planning' standard requires the auditor to plan his work to allow him to conduct an effective audit in an efficient and timely manner. The standard indicates that the audit plan should be based on a knowledge of the client's business and that the plan should be developed and revised where necessary during the audit. The 'audit evidence' standard requires the auditor to obtain sufficient appropriate evidence to enable him to draw reasonable conclusions therefrom on which to base his audit opinion. The audit evidence should be obtained through the performance of compliance and substantive procedures. The standard on 'accounting system and internal control' states that the auditor should gain an understanding of the accounting system and internal controls. In addition, he should study and evaluate the operation of those internal controls on which he wishes to rely in determining the nature, timing and extent of other audit procedures.

The standard on 'audit conclusions and reporting' consists of three paragraphs (unlike the other standards, which consist of one paragraph each). The first paragraph requires the auditor to review and assess the conclusions drawn from the audit evidence he has obtained. This review and assessment involves an overall conclusion on the presentation of the financial information. This overall conclusion must be based on a consideration of the accounting policies used, the professional and statutory requirements, the auditor's knowledge of the business and the adequate disclosure of all material matters necessary to give a true and fair view. The second paragraph requires the auditor to ensure that the audit report contains a clear written expression of his opinion on the financial information. The third paragraph requires that any qualified audit opinion should state in a clear and informative manner all the reasons for the qualification. The standard does not give examples of the exact wording to be used in qualified or unqualified audit reports. Such examples are given in AUP 3, 'Auditors' Report'. Although the examples given in AUP 3 are provided for guidance only, the suggested wording in these examples is normally used in practice, especially for audits under company legislation. Appendix 2 of AUP 3 provides the following example of an unqualified report for a single company.

Auditors' Report to the Members of XYZ Limited
In our opinion:

(a) the accompanying accounts, being the balance sheet and profit and loss account, which have been prepared under the historical cost convention stated in note . . .[1] are properly drawn up in accordance with the provisions of the Companies Act, 1961[2] and so as to give a true and fair view of:

  (i) the state of affairs of the company at . . . and of the profit (or loss) of the company for the year[3] ended on that date; and

  (ii) the other matters required by section 162 of that Act to be dealt with in the accounts;

(b) the accounting records and other records, and the registers required by that Act to be kept by the company have been properly kept in accordance with the provisions of that Act.

Address   Firm
Date   Partner
                      Chartered Accountants[4,5]

(1) Or other basis stated, for example, current cost accounting.

(2) Insert correct title of State or Territory Act or Ordinance as applicable.
(3) Substitute other period as applicable.
(4) Or 'registered public accountants' or 'public accountants'.
(5) In NSW add 'registered under the Public Accountants Registration Act, 1945, as amended'.

However, AUP 3 (issued in 1977) is currently being revised, due to the recent changes in the company legislation and in view of the principles expressed in International Auditing Guideline no. 13 (The auditor's report on financial statements).

The auditing standards laid down in Statement AUS 1 state the principles of audit conduct and performance which must be followed, and these standards are framed in very general terms. As stated earlier, the AUPs provide authoritative guidance on the procedures by which the auditing standards may be applied. The AUPs are more specific than the standards, but Statement AUS makes it clear that the practice statements do not extend or limit the application of the standards. At present there are seventeen Statements of Auditing Practice, and these are listed below.

Statements of Auditing Practice

AUP 1 Bank confirmation requests
AUP 2 Using the work of an internal auditor
AUP 3 Auditors' reports
AUP 4 Auditors' reports: historical cost – current cost
AUP 5 Existence and valuation of inventories in the context of the historical cost system
AUP 6 Solicitors' representation letters
AUP 7 Going concern
AUP 8 Audit implications of events occurring after balance date
AUP 9 Audit engagement letters
AUP 10 Planning
AUP 11 Using the work of another auditor

AUP 12 Study and evaluation of the accounting system and related internal controls in connection with an audit
AUP 13 Control of the quality of audit work
AUP 14 Audit evidence
AUP 15 Documentation
AUP 16 Fraud and error
AUP 17 Analytical review

AUP 9 to AUP 17 are each based on the relevant international auditing guideline, and were issued subsequent to the ASB's decision in 1982 to use the international auditing guidelines as a basis for Australian auditing standards and practice statements. The ASB's current work programme includes a number of topics which may result in new or revised practice statements in the near future (that is, before the end of 1984). These likely future developments are listed below.

Possible new Statements of Auditing Practice

- Audit implications of equity accounting
- Other information in documents containing audited financial information
- Audit evidence implications of managed assets and income of superannuation funds
- Retirement of auditors
- Audit implications of current cost accounting
- Related party transactions
- Using the work of an expert
- Audit implications of accounting for construction contracts
- Auditing in an EDP environment – general principles
- The effects of an EDP environment on the study and evaluation of the accounting system and related internal controls

- Computer-assisted audit techniques
- Audit sampling

Possible revisions to existing Statements of Auditing Practice

AUP 3 Auditors' reports
AUP 8 Audit implications of events occurring after
         balance date

3.4 SUMMARY

Australia has a well-developed accounting profession that
has established a mandatory set of auditing standards. There
is no limitation on the scope of these standards. There is a
series of statements of auditing practice that provide
authoritative guidance on how the auditing standards should
be applied. Government influences on financial reporting
appear to be increasing, but the recent changes have
affected accounting rather than auditing.

4 Canada

4.1 THE AUDITING AND ACCOUNTING ENVIRONMENT

The dominant influences on the Canadian accounting environment arise from legal and professional sources. The legal influence consists of the accounting measurement and disclosure requirements in the particular Act under which a Canadian company is incorporated. Early company legislation was closely modelled on the UK system (Anderson, 1977), reflecting the economic and political links of the nineteenth century. However, as these links weakened and Canada's economic and business interdependence with the US increased, the nature of company legislation shifted from a UK basis to one more closely resembling that of the US. The federal nature of the Canadian political system is a significant element of the auditing and accounting environment. The federal system has important implications for the nature of the auditing profession (discussed below). Also, the federal system has resulted in differences between the accounting requirements of the various federal and provincial Acts (OECD, 1980). However, these differences have diminished in importance since the early 1970s, and now the legislation in the provinces closely follows national legislation such as the Canada Business Corporations Act and the Ontario Securities Act.

An interesting feature of the financial reporting environment is the legal backing given to the auditing and accounting recommendations of the professional accountancy body, the Canadian Institute of Chartered Accountants (CICA). The legal status of these professional pronouncements is provided by Regulation 44 of the Canada Business Corporations Act of 1975, which states that:

> The financial statements referred to in section 149 of the Act and the auditor's report referred to in section 163 of the Act shall, except as otherwise provided by this Part, be prepared in accordance with the recommendations of the Canadian Institute of Chartered Accountants set out in the CICA *Handbook*.

This statutory provision seems to be evidence of implicit recognition by the government that the accounting profession is sufficiently responsible to be entrusted with setting detailed auditing and accounting rules. The Canadian approach permits a high degree of flexibility in changing the detailed rules, in that CICA can update the *Handbook* more easily and more frequently than the government can amend the legislation. Nevertheless, this high degree of flexibility exists in a framework of continued legal authority for the pronouncements made. As Anderson (1977) points out, this devolution of responsibility to the profession places an implicit duty on the profession to ensure that sufficient appropriate pronouncements are made on a timely basis.

The Canadian accounting profession fulfils this duty through the mechanism of two CICA committees, namely the Accounting Research Committee and the Auditing Standards Committee. A brief commentary on CICA itself is perhaps necessary before explaining the functions of these two committees. The Canadian accounting profession has a federal structure, and hence mirrors the political system. Each province has its own professional organisation, the provincial institute of chartered accountants. In Quebec, the professional organisation is not an institute but an order, namely 'L'Ordre des Comptables Agréés de Québec'. These institutes and the order are affected by provincial legislation, firstly by 'enabling' legislation which creates the institute or the order and gives it certain powers and responsibilities, and secondly by regulatory legislation, which provides restrictions on the type of person who can use the title of chartered accountant. The CICA is the national body, to which members of each provincial institute or the order automatically belong. The CICA provides a unified national organisation which can more easily represent the accounting profession's interests in dealing with central government and in the international accounting scene.

The CICA has a direct effect on financial reporting standards through its Accounting Research Committee. The board of governors of the CICA has granted this committee the authority to issue accounting recommendations, which are included in the CICA *Handbook* and which consequently have the legal authority provided by Regulation 44 of the Canada Business Corporations Act. These accounting recommendations are the end-product of a lengthy consultative procedure, designed to ensure that all interested parties are aware of and can comment on the proposals at various stages of the drafting process. The Accounting Research Committee includes representatives of various user groups such as the Canadian Council of Financial Analysts and the Financial Executives Institute of Canada, although at least two-thirds of the committee's members must belong to the CICA (and at least half of the total membership must be in public practice). In addition to this input from user groups, the CICA committee works in close contact with the relevant government body, to such an extent that Stamp and Moonitz (1978) comment that the Canadians seem to be ahead of the US in developing a working relationship between the principal enforcing agency in the public sector and the principal rule-making body in the private sector. In addition, the rule-making body knows in advance that its findings will have an authority beyond voluntary compliance on the part of auditor and client. The standard-setting process in Canada is summarised in OECD (1980) as being developed in an atmosphere of co-operation among government, industry and the accounting profession.

Reesor (1978) highlights some of the distinguishing features of the Canadian legal and financial environment in comparison with the US. His comments are based on the report of the Adams Committee (CICA, 1978). One important difference was considered to be the extent to which litigation was less common in Canada than in the US, due largely to differences in the structure of the legal system. For example, class actions and contingency fees are subject to more stringent rules in Canada. Another difference is the statutory audit requirement in Canada, requiring the shareholders of all companies to appoint an auditor. This difference is of little significance, as there are certain exemptions available for small private companies. In practice, the shareholders of such companies usually pass a resolution opting out of an audit. A further difference is the fact that most chief financial officers of Canadian companies are chartered accountants, and consequently have a common professional background and common interests with practising auditors. This is not the case in the US, where relatively few chief financial officers are CPAs.

4.2   AUDITING STANDARDS – SOURCE, HISTORY AND AUTHORITY

The present set of codified auditing standards has existed on a national basis since 1975. Prior to this, 'Instruction letters' had been issued to members of the CICA since 1968, and these were a form of codified auditing standards. The present auditing standards are found in the 'Auditing Recommendations' section of the CICA *Handbook*. Section 5100 is the Recommendation on 'Generally accepted auditing standards', which constitute the basic professional standards with which an auditor should comply when reporting upon financial statements. The CICA *Handbook* (section 5009) states that when the auditor exercises his professional judgement as to the procedures required for adherence to these basic standards, he should have regard to the other Auditing Recommendations in the *Handbook*. It is the total set of these Auditing Recommendations (not just section 5100) that is referred to in the quote from the Canada Business Corporation Act mentioned earlier. Auditing Recommendations are established by the Auditing Standards Committee, which has been authorised by the board of governors of CICA to issue recommendations on its own responsibility (compare with the Accounting Research Committee). The membership comprises sixteen chartered accountants, of whom at least ten must be in public practice, with the remainder being drawn from sources such as industry, commerce, government and the universities (CICA *Handbook,* section 5011).

The CICA *Handbook* also contains Auditing Guidelines, which are published by the steering committee of the Auditing Standards Committee. The Guidelines do not have the authority of the Recommendations, in that the Guidelines only express the opinions of the steering committee and are not actually issued by the Auditing Standards Committee itself. Guidelines may be issued when the normal consultative process of issuing Recommendations does not apply or cannot be followed sufficiently quickly, or they may be issued to indicate the steering committee's interpretations of existing Recommendations.

Canada is a member of the International Federation of Accountants (IFAC), and consequently the Auditing Standards Committee 'supports the objective of the international harmonization of . . . auditing practices' (CICA *Handbook,* section 5101.03). When the International Auditing Practices Committee (IAPC) of IFAC issues an International Auditing Guideline, the Auditing Standards Committee compares it with present Canadian practice. If significant differences exist, the Auditing Standards Committee will modify the *Handbook* unless it disagrees fundamentally with the IAPC view or unless it considers that Canadian circumstances require a different view to be taken. In any case, the CICA *Handbook* will list the IAPC Guidelines and will indicate whether adherence to present Canadian practice will ensure compliance with each IAPC Guideline.

The legal authority of the Auditing Recommendations in the CICA *Handbook* has already been explained. The CICA has no disciplinary authority, but each of the provincial institutes has an extensive range of disciplinary measures which can be used against chartered accountants who fail to comply with the *Handbook* Recommendations. Anderson (1977) explains how these disciplinary procedures operate in Ontario, which he considers to be a typical representative of the provincial disciplinary systems. This legal and professional authority indicates that the Auditing Recommendations are mandatory.

4.3 AUDITING STANDARDS – SCOPE AND CONTENT

The Auditing Recommendations in the CICA *Handbook* are intended to apply to all types of profit orientated enterprises, unless a particular Recommendation makes a specific exemption or extension (CICA *Handbook,* section 5010). However, the Recommendations do not necessarily apply to banks and insurance companies. Section 5100.03 of the *Handbook* states that the generally accepted auditing standards in section 5100.02 apply to engagements in which the objective is the expression of an opinion on financial statements. Section 5100.03 also states that certain of the generally accepted auditing standards (namely the general standard and the examination standards) are also applicable to other types of attest engagements.

The objective of an audit is defined in the introduction to the general auditing section of the *Handbook*. This says that the objective of an audit is

> to express an opinion on the fairness with which (the financial statements) present the financial position, results of operations and changes in financial position in accordance with generally accepted accounting principles, or in special circumstances another appropriate disclosed basis of accounting, consistently applied. (CICA *Handbook,* section 5000.01)

The introduction also makes it clear that the management of the enterprise is responsible for the preparation of the financial statements.

Generally accepted auditing standards are contained in the Recommendation in section 5100.02 of the CICA *Handbook*. The standards are listed under three headings, namely the general standard, examination standards and reporting standards. The general standard says that the 'examination should be performed and the report prepared by a person or persons having adequate technical training and proficiency in auditing, with due care and with an objective state of mind' (CICA *Handbook,* section 5100.02). This standard incorporates auditing concepts of competence, due care and objectivity. The standard is intended to express the spirit of the related rule (or rules) of professional conduct of each provincial institute or order (CICA *Handbook,* section 5100.04).

There are three examination standards, dealing separately with planning and supervision, internal controls and audit evidence. The first says that the audit work should be adequately planned and properly executed. It also requires proper supervision of any assistants that are employed. The second requires an appropriately organised study and evaluation of those internal controls on which the auditor subsequently relies in determining the nature, extent and timing of auditing procedures. The third examination standard says that sufficient appropriate evidence should be obtained to afford a reasonable basis to support the content of the report. Audit evidence may be obtained through such means as inspection, observation, enquiry, confirmation, computation and analysis.

There are four reporting standards, dealing separately with scope, ability to express an opinion, contents of the opinion and consistency. The first reporting standard says that the audit report should refer to the scope of the auditor's examination. The second says that the audit report should contain either an expression of opinion on the financial statements or an assertion that an opinion cannot be expressed. In the latter case, the report should explain why the auditor considers that an opinion cannot be expressed. The third reporting standard says that where an opinion is expressed, it should indicate whether the financial statements present fairly the financial position, results of operations and changes in financial position in accordance with an appropriate disclosed basis of accounting. Except in special circumstances, this basis of accounting should be generally accepted accounting principles. The third reporting standard also requires the auditor to provide in his report adequate explanation of any reservation contained in his opinion. The fourth reporting standard says that where an opinion is expressed, the audit report should indicate whether the disclosed basis of accounting has been applied in a manner consistent with that of the preceding period. If the basis or its application is not consistent, the audit report should include an adequate explanation of the nature and effect of the inconsistency.

In addition to the generally accepted auditing standards, the *Handbook* includes Auditing Recommendations on a number of other matters. In most cases these provide more detail on specific aspects of the basic principles contained in the generally accepted auditing standards. These other Recommendations are as follows:

- Knowledge of the client's business
- Documentation
- Planning and supervision
- Internal control
- Audit evidence
- Using the work of a specialist
- The auditor's standard report
- Reservations in the auditor's report
- Auditor's report when there is a change in generally accepted accounting principles or the application thereof
- Auditor's report on non-consolidated financial statements
- Other reporting matters
- Special reports

The Recommendation on the auditor's standard report gives an example of an unqualified report. Although minor changes to the wording are not prohibited, the example given is nearly always used in practice and reads as follows.

Auditor's Report

To the Shareholders of . . .
I have examined the balance sheet of . . . as at . . ., 19 . . . and the statements of income, retained earnings and changes in financial position for the year then ended. My examination was made in accordance with generally accepted auditing standards, and accordingly included such tests and other procedures as I considered necessary in the circumstances.

In my opinion, these financial statements present fairly the financial position of the company as at . . ., 19 . . . and the results of its operations and the changes in its

financial position for the year then ended in accordance
with generally accepted accounting principles applied on
a basis consistent with that of the preceding year.

City   (signed) . . .
Date   Chartered Accountant

Auditing Guidelines are included in that part of the
Handbook titled 'Accounting and Auditing Guidelines'. The
Guidelines with audit implications are as follows:

• Auditor's considerations when supplementary general
  price-level restatements are published in an annual report
• Unaudited financial statements: performance of a review
• Audit of a candidate under the Canada Elections Act
• Related party transactions and economic dependence
• Canada–United States reporting conflict with respect to
  contingencies and going concern consideration
• Auditing in an electronic data processing environment
• Auditor involvement with supplementary information
  about the effects of changing prices
• Auditor review of financial forecasts

Future auditing developments are unlikely to include
changes in the basic auditing standards. However, several
projects and research studies are being undertaken in other
areas of auditing, with the aim of revising existing *Handbook* sections and introducing new sections. These projects
include:

• Prospectuses
• Subsequent events and the date of the auditor's report
• Limited audit assurance
• Other information in documents containing audited
  financial statements
• Professional judgement
• Life assurance companies – audit reports

- Generally accepted auditing standards for federal, provincial and territorial governments
- Pension plan auditing
- Internal control in Canadian corporations
- Materiality in auditing
- Audit and control implications of data base systems
- Effect of internal control on audit strategy
- New computer control guidelines
- Small business computer systems
- Audit of a candidate under Canada Elections Act
- The audit of a small business
- New computer audit guidelines
- Audit of inventories

4.4 SUMMARY

A key feature of the Canadian financial reporting environment is the interaction between legal and professional sources in the establishment of auditing and accounting standards. Company law requires compliance with the profession's auditing and accounting standards, and so these standards are prepared by the profession but have legal authority. The profession has issued a set of auditing standards and also certain non-mandatory background material. The Canadian system of establishing auditing standards seems to be operating satisfactorily, and there are unlikely to be radical changes to this system in the near future.

5 France

5.1 THE AUDITING AND ACCOUNTING ENVIRONMENT

The main influences on the accounting environment in France have arisen from government sources rather than from the accounting profession. The strong government influence can be traced back to the introduction of the commercial code in 1807. The government perceives the financial reporting framework to be a key factor in formulating and implementing national economic policy. This is evidenced by the government's emphasis on a standardised chart of accounts (which is used as a basis for collecting macroeconomic data), and also by the influence of tax laws on financial reporting. The relative weakness of the accounting profession is partly due to patterns of share ownership. France (unlike the UK and the US) does not have a tradition of large numbers of widely-held companies, and consequently there have been fewer demands for an accounting profession that formulates and monitors external financial reporting rules.

The principal government influence is *Le Plan Comptable Général*, which is the basic accounting rule-book in France. It contains valuation principles as well as a detailed list of disclosure rules (Percival *et al.*, 1982). The *Plan Comptable* was originally developed in the 1940s and was based on the German requirements. A revised version was issued in 1957. Another major revision has been drafted in recent years, and was finally approved in 1983. Minor amendments are made by a process of continuous updating, based on the pronouncements of the administering body, the *Conseil National de la Comptabilité (CNC)*. The *CNC* is responsible to the Ministry for Economic Affairs (Beeny, 1976). The *CNC* has over 100 members, representing a variety of preparers and users of financial statements. The *CNC* members include accountants, industrialists, bankers, academics and government representatives. All these interest groups can therefore have an indirect influence on the preparation and interpretation of the codified accounting standards contained in the *Plan Comptable*.

Company laws as such have been less influential than the *Plan Comptable*. The Law of 24 July 1966 includes some disclosure and measurement requirements. The commercial code deals with accounting records rather than with reporting.

Tax laws have had a significant impact on corporate financial reporting in France. Items such as depreciation and certain provisions can only be included in the tax accounts to the extent that they are included in the financial accounts. Consequently, the financial accounts may be influenced more by the desire to reduce the company's tax bill than by the desire to reflect the underlying economic events.

An important quasi-governmental influence is the *Commission des Opérations de Bourse (COB)*, a regulatory agency similar to the Securities and Exchange Commission in the US. The *COB* was established in 1967 to supervise the information being disclosed by companies listed (or seeking a listing) on the stock exchange. Membership of *COB* comprises government-appointed representatives from industry, the accounting profession and the government itself. If the *COB* notes any omissions or errors in the financial statements of listed companies, it can require the company to amend and republish the information. It can also apply the ultimate sanction of delisting. The *COB* has been involved in the revision of the *Plan Comptable*. Two of the main aims of the *COB* have been to persuade companies first, to publish consolidated accounts, and secondly, to make their financial statements both informative and attractive (Beeny, 1976).

The main impact of the accounting profession on reporting requirements has been through its representatives on *CNC* and *COB*. The accounting profession is also involved in advising companies as to how the legal reporting requirements should be complied with. The government domination of the standard-setting scene has left little room for the professional accounting bodies to develop their own authoritative pronouncements. The professional bodies have issued a number of opinions and recommendations on accounting matters, but these statements are generally interpretations of the legal requirements.

The accounting profession has a greater influence on the auditing environment than on the accounting environment. However, government influence in the auditing environment is more noticeable in France than in (for example) the UK or the US.

The Law of 24 July 1966 requires that all public companies, and all private companies with share capital in excess of FF300 000, must appoint a statutory auditor *(commissaire aux comptes)*. Public companies that are listed on the stock exchange or that have share capital in excess of FF5 000 000 must appoint at least two statutory auditors. The law provides that statutory auditors must audit the company's accounting records and must verify *la régularité et la sincérité* of the company's accounts. Although *la régularité et la sincérité* may be translated as 'truth and fairness', the underlying concept may not be the same as the UK 'true and fair' concept, due to differences in the underlying legal and business cultures. A better translation might be 'correctness and fairness'. The law provides that the statutory auditors must report certain specified information to the shareholders. The law also requires the statutory auditors to notify the Public Prosecutor of any criminal acts of the company's directors that come to their attention.

Statutory auditors belong to the *Compagnie Nationale des Commissaires aux Comptes (CNCC),* one of the two professional accounting bodies. The *CNCC* was established in 1969 by a government decree regulating the statutory auditing profession. The other professional body is the *Ordre des Experts Comptables et des Comptables Agréés (OECCA),* established in 1942. *Experts comptables* form the upper tier of *OECCA,* with a higher level of qualifications than the *comptables agréés,* who are primarily book-keepers. The qualification of *comptables agréés* is no longer being granted, and the category will eventually be phased out. The *OECCA* is regulated by a 1945 government ordinance, which conferred on *OECCA* a monopoly of all public accounting work other than statutory audits (Welch-man, 1983). However, *experts comptables* lose their right to that title if they leave the public accounting profession (for example, to work in industry). The *OECCA* is larger than *CNCC,* due to the number of *comptables agréés* who belong to *OECCA.* Although most members of *CNCC* are also members of *OECCA,* there is a history of disputes between the two bodies. This atmosphere seems to have improved in the 1980s, although Mantle (1983) considers that progress towards a unified body will be hampered by political and factional constraints.

Statutory auditors are governed by strict legal require-ments concerning their independence. If they have been appointed as statutory auditors of a company, they are not permitted to receive any remuneration from that company for services other than the statutory audit. This prohibits them from providing management consultancy services, tax advice or general accounting services to their audit clients. Consequently, the business of *experts comptables* consists of some statutory auditing and some consultancy, tax and accounting services to non-audit clients. *Commissaires aux comptes* are restricted to statutory audits unless they are also *experts comptables*.

There have been two interesting recent developments in the French accounting profession. One is the impact of the *Association Française pour le Développement de l'Audit (AFDA)*, established in 1982 by a number of indigenous auditing firms who resented the perceived intrusion of the international auditing firms. The main stated aim of *AFDA* is to raise the quality of auditing, but its exact role is not yet clear. The international auditing firms are mostly staffed (and partnered) by French nationals, who seem to have good grounds for criticising *AFDA's* arbitrary distinction between 'French' and 'non-French' firms. *AFDA* has also been criticised by a number of small French firms, who consider that *AFDA* is attempting to establish an élite of large French firms (Welchman, 1983).

The second recent development is a 1982 government report on the future of the accounting profession (Mantle, 1983). This proposed the setting-up of a new independent body responsible for regulating statutory auditors. It also proposes a new national accounting institute, which would be responsible for setting accounting standards. The *CNCC* is (perhaps not surprisingly) strongly against the first proposal, but otherwise is in general agreement with the report. The report is generating much debate within government and the profession, but radical changes are unlikely to occur in the short term.

5.2 AUDITING STANDARDS – SOURCE, HISTORY AND AUTHORITY

Both the *CNCC* and the *OECCA* have issued auditing standards *(recommandations)*. The *CNCC* standards were issued in 1980 (*CNCC*, 1980), and replaced an earlier series of standards issued in 1971. The new standards were issued in response to a number of changes in the auditing environment. For example, the new *Plan Comptable* was being developed. Also, computerised accounting systems were rapidly becoming more common. Another change in the auditing environment was the increasing interest in French financial statements by international user groups. This led to the *CNCC* taking account of international auditing standards.

The *CNCC* standards are essentially recommendations rather than requirements. This contrasts with the position in the UK or the US, for example, where the members of the relevant professional bodies must comply with the UK or US auditing standards. Although the *CNCC* standards are not mandatory, they do constitute authoritative guidance as to how the professional body considers that its members should conduct a normal audit. The *CNCC* recognises that the standards must satisfy two conflicting requirements. First, they must be sufficiently general to allow individual auditors freedom of choice in determining specific audit practices. Secondly, they must be sufficiently detailed to allow users of audit reports (including the courts) to assess the quality of the auditor's performance. Consequently, it seems that although the *CNCC* standards are not mandatory, the courts and other disciplinary bodies may take the standards into account in determining acceptable auditing conduct.

The *OECCA* standards are found in a series of *révisions comptables*. This series is one of several types of *recommandations* issued by the *Comité permanent des diligences normales,* an *OECCA* committee that contains a number of *experts comptables* and also representatives from industry, government, universities and the *COB*. This committee has also issued *recommandations* on accounting principles and on the disclosure of financial information to the public. The *OECCA* standards are recommendations rather than requirements. All *OECCA* members are *expected* to comply with the standards (Collins and Pham, 1983), but there are

no sanctions for non-compliance. Because the *CNCC* is the
body responsible for statutory auditors, the next section
concentrates on the *CNCC* auditing standards and makes
only brief reference to the *OECCA* standards.

5.3 AUDITING STANDARDS – SCOPE AND CONTENT

The *CNCC* auditing standards include personal standards,
performance standards and reporting standards. The personal standards apply to the audits of all societies and
organisations where there is a legal requirement for a
commissaire aux comptes to carry out an audit. The
performance standards apply to all audits whose purpose is
the verification of the *régularité et sincérité* of the financial
information. The scope of the reporting standards is not
specified in the *CNCC* standards but is considered to be the
same as for the personal standards. The *CNCC* standards
also include recommendations relating to specific legal
obligations (most of which arise from the 1966 Law). These
recommendations are mostly detailed guidelines as to how
auditors should interpret the specific legal requirements.
The following paragraphs deal with the personal, performance and reporting standards only.

The section on personal standards begins by describing
certain general principles, most of which are derived from
the auditing requirements in the 1966 Law. In most cases
these general principles are dealt with in more detail in the
subsequent standards. This introductory section on general
principles is followed by the set of four personal standards,
entitled *Recommandations à Caractère Général*. The first
personal standard says that the auditor should be, and be
seen to be, independent. The auditor should maintain an
attitude of mind that allows him to perform the audit with
integrity and objectivity, and in addition, he should be free

of any relationship that might be interpreted as adversely affecting his integrity and objectivity. The second personal standard is a competence standard, and refers to the detailed legal and professional requirements for the education and training of *commissaires aux comptes*. The standard also says that auditors should keep up-to-date with relevant matters once they have qualified, and should ensure that their assistants have a level of competence appropriate to the work they are required to perform. The third personal standard deals with the quality of the work performed and with delegation. The standard requires the auditor to exercise due professional care in order to achieve a sufficient level of quality in his work. Also, although some of the auditor's duties cannot be delegated to assistants, some can be so delegated, in which case the auditor should ensure that his assistants also achieve a sufficient level of quality in their audit work. The fourth personal standard says that the auditor should not disclose any confidential information that he acquires during the audit, and he should ensure that his assistants are aware of, and comply with, the confidentiality rules. All of the personal standards refer to specific legal and professional requirements on the particular topic. Consequently, although each personal standard is only a recommendation, there is in fact a body of legal and professional rules on the topic that *must* be complied with.

There are nine performance standards, five dealing with the nature of the audit work and four dealing with the organisation of the audit work. The first performance standard says that the auditor should acquire a general knowledge of the business whose financial statements are being audited. This will give him a better understanding of those factors that may have a significant effect on the financial statements. The auditor should take his knowledge of the business into account when planning the audit, in particular by identifying those audit areas that will require special attention. The second performance standard says that the auditor should analyse the enterprise's internal control system, in order to understand its strengths and weaknesses and in order to determine the nature, extent and timing of his audit tests. The third performance standard says that as a result of the conclusions drawn from his study of the internal controls, the auditor should develop an audit programme that will allow him to form an opinion on the information in the financial statements. The audit programme should test whether the company has complied with the particular legal requirements (for example, those of the *Plan Comptable)*. The audit programme should also include tests that verify the existence and ownership of the assets in the financial statements, and that verify that the liabilities are those of the company. The fourth performance standard says that the auditor should obtain sufficient audit evidence to allow him to certify the *régularité et sincérité* of the financial statements. The audit evidence should be sufficient in terms of quality and of quantity. The fifth performance standard says that the auditor should perform a review of the financial statements. This review should determine whether the financial statements reflect the company's state of affairs and results of operations in a manner that is *sincère et régulière*. The review should take into account the knowledge that the auditor has acquired as a result of his other audit tests and procedures.

The remaining four performance standards deal with the organisation of the audit work. The sixth performance standard refers to the personal nature of the audit appointment. It says that although the auditor can delegate some work to assistants or to independent experts, he retains sole responsibility for the performance of the audit, and the audit opinion. The seventh performance standard deals with audit planning. The auditor should perform his audit as efficiently and effectively as possible, taking into account the legal requirements and any other relevant recommendations. The eighth performance standard says that the auditor should exercise an appropriate degree of supervision over any audit work that he has delegated to assistants or to independent experts. The ninth performance standard says that the auditor should record the audit tests performed and the conclusions reached.

The *CNCC* reporting standards must be viewed in the context of the legal reporting requirements. The statutory auditor is required by law to give certain information to management and certain information to shareholders (Deloitte Haskins & Sells, 1980). He must provide management with details of audit tests performed, amendments that the auditor considers should be made to the financial statements, details of errors and irregularities found and conclusions on the results of the year. The report may be given orally or in writing. The auditor must provide the shareholders with a general report and a special report. The general report must give details of audit tests and (if applicable) explain the reasons as to why he is unable to certify the *régularité et sincérité* of the financial statements. The general report must also include details of changes in accounting measurement and disclosure practices, errors and irregularities noted during the audit, and certain matters relating to share acquisitions. The special report covers transactions with directors and related parties.

Although the law requires the auditor to include specific items in his reports to the shareholders, the law does not specify the precise form or wording of the audit report. The *CNCC* considered that a recommended form of audit report would benefit auditors and also the users of audit reports. Consequently, the *CNCC* issued a set of reporting standards relating to the general report to shareholders. The *CNCC* will subsequently issue reporting standards for the special report.

The reporting standards say that the auditor should certify the correctness and fairness of the financial statements. He should state in his report that he has complied with the profession's auditing standards. Where the auditor cannot certify the correctness and fairness of the financial statements, or where he expresses reservations, he should clearly state the reasons for this and, if possible, should quantify the amounts involved.

These reporting standards are supported by a number of guidelines that explain in more detail the recommendations in the reporting standards. The standards include an example of an unqualified audit report and examples of qualified audit reports. The model unqualified audit report is given below.

In performing the duties entrusted to me by your general meeting of . . ., I have pleasure in presenting my report on the financial statements for the accounting period from . . . to . . .

(1) *Certification*

(a) I have audited the financial statements of your company for this accounting period. *(The auditor may include here details of any errors and irregularities not leading to a qualified report.)*

(b) I have audited the fairness of the information relating to the financial situation of the company, as given in the documents sent to the shareholders or laid before them in general meeting. *(The auditor may include here additional remarks or information as appropriate.)*

(c) On the basis of the audit work that I have carried out in accordance with the profession's auditing standards, I consider myself able to certify that the stocktaking lists, the trading account, the profit and loss account and the balance sheet as presented on pages . . . of this report are correct and fair.

(2) *Information*

In accordance with the law, I bring the following facts

to your attention. *(These will relate to matters such as share acquisitions that the law requires the auditor to include in his report.)*

> Place
> Date
> Signature

Qualified audit reports can take the form of either a certification with reservations or a refusal to certify. A certification with reservations should describe the areas about which the auditor has reservations, and should then go on to state that except for these matters, the auditor certifies the correctness and fairness of the relevant information. A refusal to certify will arise in two cases. The first case is where there are areas of fundamental error or disagreement such that the auditor considers that the financial statements are not correct and fair. The second case is where the scope of the audit has been limited (by the directors or by circumstances) in such a way as to prevent the auditor from forming an opinion or the financial statements.

As mentioned in the previous section, the *OECCA* has issued a set of auditing standards. These consist of a series of *recommandations* as listed below:

- Standards of auditing
- Audit of inventories
- Confirmation procedures
- Audit of investments and marketable securities
- Audit of consolidated statements
- Audit of statutory business combinations
- Computer-assisted audit techniques
- Materiality
- Audit of overheads
- Bank confirmations

5.4 SUMMARY

The French auditing and accounting environment is dominated by legal influences. There are two professional bodies,
the *CNCC* and the *OECCA*, both of which have issued
auditing standards. These standards are more in the nature
of guidelines than mandatory requirements. The recent
CNCC reporting standards should result in greater uniformity in auditors' general reports to shareholders. However,
the auditor is required by law to report on several specific
aspects of the company's activities, and such details will vary
according to the particular circumstances of the company.
Consequently, it is likely that audit reports will not become
as standardised as they are in (for example) the UK or the
US.

6 West Germany

6.1 THE AUDITING AND ACCOUNTING ENVIRONMENT

The auditing and accounting environment in Germany is influenced predominantly by government sources. These sources include company law, the commercial code and tax regulations. The accounting profession is relatively small and has had little influence on establishing accounting principles and standards. However, the profession has issued a set of auditing standards.

The German Stock Corporation Law of 1965 (referred to below as the 1965 Law) is the main government influence on financial reporting. An English translation has been published by Mueller and Galbraith (1976). The 1965 law applies to all public limited companies *(Aktiengesellschaft)*. It includes detailed rules for the valuation of assets and liabilities and for the format of the financial statements. It also governs the contents of the 'management report' *(Geschäftsberichts)*, which forms part of the annual financial report. Section 149 of the 1965 Law states that the annual financial statements must conform to *Grundsätzen ordnungsmässiger Buchführung,* referred to below as *GoB. GoB* is translated by Mueller and Galbraith as 'proper accounting principles'. However, Macharzina (1981) indicates that *GoB* refers to a set of bookkeeping or accounting rules rather than to a set of accounting concepts or principles. In any case, the *GoB* do not arise from a single source but rather are found in company law, the commercial code and the tax regulations. The civil courts are ultimately responsible for interpreting the meaning of *GoB*. However, these courts rarely involve themselves in accounting issues (Wysocki, 1983). The tax courts have been more active in determining the precise nature of *GoB*.

The commercial code dates from 1897. It contains general valuation rules as well as certain bookkeeping and administrative provisions. Although the commercial code is the oldest government influence on financial reporting, it is now considered to be less significant than company law or the tax regulations.

The tax regulations have a significant influence on the accounting environment. The financial accounts form the basis of the tax accounts, and most tax concessions are only available if the deductions or valuations are also reflected in the financial accounts. This can lead to a situation where the management is more concerned with reducing the company's tax liability than with ensuring that the financial statements properly reflect the underlying economic position and performance of the company. Another important tax influence is the existence of the 'tax audit' that is performed by the tax authorities on each year's accounts of a large company (Beeny, 1975). The tax audit may be delayed for a number of years, but nevertheless the existence of these thorough checks is considered to be an important factor in management's attitude towards compliance with the accounting and tax legislation.

The German accounting profession (see below) has had little direct influence on the development of accounting requirements. The professional body has a committee (the *Hauptfachauschuss*) that issues pronouncements on measurement and disclosure issues. These pronouncements are not formally binding and consequently are more in the nature of recommendations than requirements. In most cases these pronouncements are considered to represent best practice and so would be interpreted by the courts as forming part of *GoB*. However, some pronouncements (notably the ones on leasing and on pension plans) have met with little support outside the profession (Wysocki, 1983). These instances emphasise the lack of sanctions available to the professional body in attempting to ensure compliance with its accounting pronouncements.

Company law has an important impact on the auditing environment as well as on the accounting environment. An audit is required for all public limited companies and for other enterprises meeting certain size criteria. These criteria are laid down in the 1969 German Law on the Accounting by Major Enterprises other than Stock Corporations (Mueller and Galbraith, 1976), which extends the accounting and auditing requirements of the 1965 Law to large non-public companies. When the EEC Fourth Directive is implemented into German company law, the audit requirement will be extended to include all private limited companies.

The 1965 Law sets out the basic rights and duties of the auditor of a public limited company. The scope of the audit includes the management report as well as the balance sheet, profit and loss account and notes. Section 166 of the 1965 Law requires the auditor to submit a long-form report to the company's board of management. This report should include an analysis and explanation of the headings in the financial statements. It should state whether the company's accounting records, financial statements and management report comply with the legislation. The auditor must also report on any facts that he is aware of that either endanger the current position or future development of the company, or involve serious breaches of the law or articles by the company's management. This long-form report is not made available to the shareholders, although providers of loan capital, such as banks, will often demand (and receive) a copy. The 1965 Law requires the auditor to attach a short-form report to the financial statements. This attestation *(Bestätigungsvermerk)* is very brief and deals only with compliance with the law (see next section).

The 1965 Law states that only a *Wirtschaftsprüfer (WP)* or associations of *WPs* may become auditors. An association of *WPs (Wirtschaftsprüfungsgesellschaft)* can either be a partnership or a limited company. Either the members of the board of management, the managing directors or the partners with unlimited personal liability must be *WPs*. The German auditing profession therefore consists of the 5000 or so *WPs* and associations of *WPs*. The auditing profession is regulated by the 1961 Law Regulating the Profession of *Wirtschaftsprüfer (Wirtschaftsprüferordnung* or *WPO)*. An English translation of this is available *(Wirtschaftsprüfer-kammer,* 1981). The 1961 Law is a uniform federal law which replaced the existing individual state legislation. The 1961 Law requires all *WPs* to be members of the Chamber of Auditors *(Wirtschaftsprüferkammer)*. This is a federal regulatory body under the aegis of the Federal Ministry of Economics. The 1961 Law sets out the detailed requirements for qualification as a *WP* (ICAEW, 1980). The qualification procedures are long and arduous, and *WPs* rarely qualify before the age of thirty-five (Beeny, 1975). Although the federal government is the source of the qualification requirements, it is the individual states *(Länder)* who confer the *WP* qualification on successful candidates. The qualification conferred by one state is equally valid in all states.

The private sector professional body is the *Institut der Wirtschaftsprüfer in Deutschland e.V (IdW)*. This is a voluntary organisation, but nearly all *WPs* become members. The *IdW* concentrates mainly on technical matters and on promoting the interests of the auditing profession. This is a much narrower role than that occupied by the statutory Chamber of Auditors, which is responsible for all aspects of the auditing profession.

Membership of the Chamber of Auditors is restricted to

practising auditors (or audit firms). If a *WP* were to leave auditing and become (for example) an accountant in industry, then he would lose his *WP* qualification. Consequently, financial managers and directors do not belong to the *IdW*, and so the professional body has no direct influence over the preparers of financial statements (in contrast to the UK, for example, where financial directors frequently belong to one of the professional accountancy bodies).

Germany has a number of important stock exchanges, the most important being in Frankfurt. However, the stock exchanges are not considered to have a significant influence on financial reporting requirements or practices.

A standard chart of accounts is no longer prescribed by law in Germany (Percival *et al.*, 1982). However, a recommended chart of accounts is published by the employers' association, the *Bundesverband der Deutschen Industrie*. The classifications in this chart are designed to produce the necessary information to comply with the financial statements formats required by the 1965 Law.

6.2 AUDITING STANDARDS – SOURCE, HISTORY AND AUTHORITY

Auditing standards in Germany arise from two sources. The Chamber of Auditors issues personal standards, and the *IdW* issues field-work standards and reporting standards. Section 57(2) of the 1961 Law gives the Chamber of Auditors responsibility for 'laying down in rules the general concept with regard to questions concerning the practice of the profession of *WPs*'. To fulfil this responsibility, the Chambers of Auditors has issued rules for the professional conduct of its members. The first set of such rules was issued in 1964, and the current amended version was issued in 1977 *(Wirtschaftsprüferkammer,* 1981). The foreword to the

Chamber of Auditors' rules of professional conduct says that the rules are intended to interpret and clarify the professional duties laid down in the 1961 Law. These professional duties include the obligation to observe the principles set out in the rules of professional conduct. The 1961 Law sets out four sanctions which the disciplinary court may use in cases of breach of professional duty. These sanctions are warnings, reprimands, fines, or exclusion from the profession. The rules are accompanied by interpreting statements, which are intended to give guidance on how the rules should be applied in practice.

The *IdW* has issued auditing pronouncements since 1934. In 1977 the *IdW* issued revised versions of the field-work standards and reporting standards *(Institut der Wirtschaftsprüfer, 1977)*. The foreword to these standards says that a *WP* is 'bound to' comply with these standards. However, in exceptional cases he is allowed to depart from these standards, but only if such departures can be justified. The *IdW* auditing standards are referred to indirectly in the rules of professional conduct of the Chamber of Auditors. An interpreting statement of one of those rules says that *WPs* should carefully consider whether the principles contained in any *IdW* statement are applicable in their particular circumstances.

6.3 AUDITING STANDARDS – SCOPE AND CONTENT

There is no restriction on the scope of the auditing standards. Both the Chamber of Auditors' rules of professional conduct and the *IdW's* field-work and reporting standards apply whenever a *WP* is carrying out a professional assignment. Consequently, a user of a *WP's* audit report can assume that these auditing standards applied to the *WP*.

The Chamber of Auditors' rules of professional conduct are grouped under the following nine headings:

(1) Independence and freedom from prejudice
(2) Conscientiousness
(3) Personal responsibility
(4) Professional confidentiality
(5) Impartiality
(6) Ethical behaviour
(7) Incompatible activities
(8) Public announcements and protection of assignments
(9) Signing of opinions and audit certificates

The key points of these rules are as follows. The first rule requires the *WP* to be, and be seen to be, free of any influence or ties that might affect his independence. The interpreting statement makes it clear that this rule does not prevent the *WP* from advising his audit client on financial and tax matters. However, if a *WP* prepares a set of financial statements he is not permitted to audit them (although he is permitted to audit financial statements if he only *assisted* in their preparation). The fourth rule requires the auditor to maintain confidentiality in respect of all matters that come to his attention through his professional work. He must not use such information for his own purposes, nor must he disclose it to others without authorisation. The eighth rule prohibits the *WP* from advertising. This rule is accompanied by the longest interpreting statement, which describes in detail the principles to be applied with regard to public announcements and the obtaining of professional assignments.

The *IdW* standards deal with field-work and with reporting. There are two sets of reporting standards, one for the long-form report to the board of management and one for the attestation issued with the financial statements.

The *IdW* standards of field-work are contained in Statement 1/1977 of the *IdW*, entitled 'Generally accepted standards for the audit of financial statements'. This defines the objectives of an audit as being to determine whether the accounting records, financial statements and management report comply with the law and with the company's statutes, and whether within this framework they permit as accurate a view as possible of the financial position and results of operations. This echoes the requirements of section 149 of the 1965 Law, which says that a company's financial statements shall give as accurate a view of the company's financial position and results as is possible within the framework of the valuation rules.

There are ten standards of field-work. The first standard requires the auditor to examine compliance with the law and with the company's statutes (insofar as they relate to the financial statements in question). This examination is considered to be the most important part of the audit.

The second standard of field-work requires the auditor to examine whether the financial statements comply with generally accepted accounting principles. The standard notes that the principles come from a variety of sources, such as court decisions, accounting literature and *IdW* pronouncements, and recognises that these principles may change over time. The standard requires the auditor to keep up-to-date with developments in this area.

The third standard of field-work refers to adherence to statements and professional pronouncements. The standard requires the auditor to consider carefully whether the principles in the *IdW* statements and technical opinions should be applied in the financial statements. If the auditor accepts non-compliance with these principles, he may be at a disadvantage in any subsequent professional disciplinary proceedings or claims for damages.

The fourth standard deals with planning and supervision of the audit. In addition to proper audit planning and an appropriate degree of supervision, there must be a critical review by the auditor of the findings and conclusions of his assistants.

The fifth standard deals with the general nature and scope of audit procedures. This standard requires the auditor to determine the nature and scope of his audit procedures in such a way as to enable him to make an informed judgement on the compliance of the financial statements with the law and with generally accepted accounting principles. The auditor must determine the nature and scope of his audit procedures in a conscientious manner and with due professional care, having regard to factors such as the company's accounting system, materiality and the probability of error.

The sixth standard deals with the audit of the internal control system. The auditor must take an informed view of the role and significance of the audit of the internal control system, and plan his audit procedures accordingly. The standard says that the audit and evaluation of the internal control system allows the auditor to determine the type and scope of his audit procedures in an appropriate manner. The standard does not specifically state that the auditor must record and evaluate the internal control system, but this seems to be the implication.

The seventh standard deals with the verification of the existence of assets and liabilities. The general rule is that the auditor must examine whether the type, quantity and value of all assets and liabilities are properly stated. The specific rules state that the auditor should obtain direct confirmation of a sample of debtor and creditor balances. Attendance at the client's stocktaking is recommended but is not mandatory.

The eighth standard deals with the acceptance of audit results and work of third parties. Although the auditor is solely responsible for his report and opinion, he may rely to some extent on the work of other parties. The degree of reliance will depend on the auditor's assessment of the competence and professional qualifications of the third party.

The ninth standard requires the auditor to obtain a representation letter from his audit client. This is in addition to, not a substitute for, the specific audit procedures. The *IdW* has published sample representation letters.

The tenth standard states that the auditor must adequately document the nature, scope and results of his audit procedures. This information must be documented in working papers that are comprehensible and are systematically filed.

The first set of the *IdW* reporting standards is contained in Statement 2/1977 of the *IdW,* entitled 'Generally accepted reporting standards for the audit of financial statements'. This deals with the long-form report to the board of management. There are three general reporting standards. The standard of completeness requires the auditor to include in the audit report all matters required by law or contract, and also all material findings of the audit. The standard of truth requires the auditor to be satisfied that the content of the audit report is in accordance with the facts. The standard of clarity requires the audit report to be presented in understandable and unequivocal terms.

There are also a number of specific reporting standards. Most of these consist of the legal reporting requirements laid down in section 166 of the 1965 Law. In addition, the auditor is required to state that he has conducted the audit in accordance with the generally accepted standards for the audit of financial statements (*IdW* Statement 1/1977). The audit report should summarise the audit results, and should substantiate a qualification or disclaimer of opinion (if applicable).

The second set of the *IdW* reporting standards is contained in Statement 3/1977 of the *IdW,* entitled 'Standards for the issue of audit opinions'. This consists of a general standard and a number of specific standards dealing with types of audit opinions. The general standard makes it clear that the opinion only relates to compliance of the financial statements with the law and with generally accepted accounting principles. No opinion is given on the company's economic position or on the company's management. The opinion should be an overall conclusion, based on the auditor's evaluation of the materiality of the individual conclusions.

The text of an unqualified opinion is prescribed by section 167 of the 1965 Law and this is reproduced in the reporting standard as follows:

> The accounting, the annual financial statements and the management report, which I (we) have examined with due care, comply with law and with the company's statutes.

Section 167 says that an unqualified opinion should be issued if, on the basis of the final results of the audit, no exceptions can be raised. Immaterial exceptions would not preclude the issue of an unqualified opinion.

A qualified opinion should be issued if material exceptions arise from the final results of the audit. Exceptions could arise from a number of sources, such as deficiencies in the accounting records, departures from the valuation or disclosure principles laid down by law or the company's statutes, or from insufficient explanations and presentations to the auditor. A qualified opinion should be issued as long as an affirmation can be reached and the exceptions relate to identifiable areas. A qualified opinion should clearly state the fact of and reasons for the qualification, and should include the word 'exception'. The positive part of the opinion should not stand on its own. If practicable, the amount at issue should be quantified. If affirmation on the major accounting areas is not possible, the auditor should issue a disclaimer of opinion.

Additions to standard opinions are desirable or required in cases where no exceptions have arisen but the auditor considers an additional statement necessary. Such additions may represent reservations or explanations. Qualifications of the opinion must be clearly stated as such, and must not give the impression of being additions to the standard opinion.

6.4 SUMMARY

The German auditing and accounting environment is dominated by legal influences. There is a statutory Chamber of Auditors, to which all professional accountants must belong. There is also a private sector professional body, membership of which is voluntary. The statutory body has issued a set of personal standards, and the private sector body has issued field-work standards and reporting standards. There is a set of reporting standards dealing with the long-form report to management, and a set of reporting standards dealing with the audit opinion attached to the financial statements.

7   Japan

7.1   THE AUDITING AND ACCOUNTING ENVIRONMENT

The government is the most significant influence on the Japanese financial reporting environment. Government influences arise from three distinct sources, namely the commercial code, the Securities and Exchange Law and the tax regulations. These three sources have differing attitudes and objectives with respect to financial reporting, and there is little overall co-ordination or control. As a consequence, there is no single 'government influence' on Japanese financial reporting, but rather a number of (sometimes conflicting) government influences.

The first source of government influence is the commercial code, which is administered by the Ministry of Justice and which applies to all *kabushiki kaisha* (similar to public limited companies in the UK). The nature of the commercial code reflects the legal background of the personnel in the Ministry of Justice, in that there is a strong emphasis on the protection of creditors. This is considered to be at least as important as the protection of shareholders, and hence the commercial code tends to concentrate on asset valuation rather than income measurement.

The second government influence is the Securities and Exchange Law, which is administered by the Ministry of Finance and which applies only to those *kabushiki kaisha* that are publicly traded. Only 2800 or so of the 767 000 *kabushiki kaisha* come within the scope of the Securities and Exchange Law. These 2800 companies have to prepare two sets of financial statements, one complying with the requirements of the Securities and Exchange Law and one complying with the requirements of the commercial code. The Securities and Exchange Law was strongly influenced by the Securities Act and the Securities Exchange Act of the United States, whereas the commercial code was initially influenced by German company law. The Ministry of Finance is responsible for establishing accounting and auditing standards, and it is advised in this by the Business Accounting Deliberation Council (BADC). The members of the BADC come from a variety of backgrounds, such as industry, commerce, government, the accounting profession and the universities. The BADC prepares accounting standards in response to specific requests from the Ministry of Finance, who then publish the standards. All financial reports prepared in accordance with the Securities and Exchange Law must follow these accounting standards. Because the Securities and Exchange Law only applies to publicly traded companies (which tend to be those of the greatest economic significance), the requirements of the Securities and Exchange Law and the BADC are generally more rigorous and more advanced than those of the commercial code.

The third government influence arises from the tax regulations. Certain deductions of expenses (such as depreciation and bad debt allowances) are only permitted for tax purposes if they are passed through the company's statutory accounts prepared under the commercial code.

The Ministry of Finance seems to be becoming a stronger influence on Japanese financial reporting than the Ministry of Justice. This may result in a move away from the 'legal' approach towards a more 'economic' approach to financial reporting requirements. That is to say, presenting a realistic picture of the underlying economic events may become more important than strictly complying with the letter of the law. Another change likely to occur is a greater degree of harmonisation of the three government influences (instigated primarily by the BADC).

The Japanese accounting profession is of relatively recent origin and has had little significant impact on financial reporting requirements and practices. The professional body is the Japanese Institute of Certified Public Accountants (JICPA), with a total membership of approximately 8400. Membership of the professional body is mandatory for all certified public accountants (CPAs) in Japan. The JICPA issues recommendations and guidelines on accounting matters. Although these are described as recommendations, they are actually more in the nature of requirements, particularly for companies reporting to the Ministry of Finance under the Securities and Exchange Law. The reason for this is that the Ministry of Finance would consider non-compliance with the JICPA statements to be a departure from acceptable accounting practices, and if such departures were material then the Ministry would require the financial statements to be amended. However, although the JICPA statements are supported by this powerful sanction, the statements themselves tend to deal with relatively minor matters. The main reporting issues are dealt with in the BADC standards. The relative weakness of the accounting profession is further indicated by the fact that it is the BADC, not the JICPA, which issues auditing standards and guidelines. There is however an indirect professional influence on financial reporting through the membership of individual CPAs on the BADC. Very few CPAs hold senior financial positions in industry or commerce, so the profession has little influence on the preparers of financial information. In any case, Japanese financial managers have developed few innovative financial reporting practices.

There are a number of stock exchanges in Japan, the principal one being situated in Tokyo. However, the stock exchanges are government-regulated, not self-regulated, and they impose no reporting requirements in addition to the Securities and Exchange Law. This emphasises the key role of the government in the accounting environment.

The auditing environment is also strongly influenced by the government, primarily through the Ministry of Finance and the BADC. Financial statements prepared under the Securities and Exchange Law must be audited by an independent CPA or audit corporation *(kansa hojin)*. An audit corporation is similar in many ways to an accounting partnership in the UK or the US. The objective of the audit is to determine whether the financial statements are presented fairly and in accordance with generally accepted accounting principles. Financial statements prepared under the commercial code must be reported on by a *kansa yaku*, which is usually translated as a statutory auditor (or statutory examiner). The statutory auditor's role under the commercial code differs fundamentally from that of the independent auditor under the Securities and Exchange Law. The statutory auditor reports on whether the financial statements required by the commercial code have been properly prepared in accordance with the code. The concept of 'present fairly' does not apply. Although the statutory auditor must not be a director or employee of the company, he is not independent in the Western sense, as a statutory auditor normally works full-time for only one company. There is usually only one statutory auditor per company, and as he rarely has any staff the extent of his examination is limited. The statutory auditor need not be a CPA. However, companies capitalised at over 500 million yen or with liabilities over 20 billion yen must also have an independent audit conducted by a CPA or audit corporation.

7.2 AUDITING STANDARDS – SOURCE, HISTORY AND AUTHORITY

The BADC is the source of the main set of codified auditing standards. This codified set of auditing standards includes not only general standards, field-work standards and reporting standards, but also a detailed list of auditing procedures. The BADC auditing standards are discussed in more detail in the next section. The Ministry of Finance has issued additional rules governing specific reporting issues, and has also laid down certain independence rules. The JICPA has issued a number of auditing statements on an *ad hoc* basis. The JICPA statements are published in the form of guidelines and tend to deal with specific auditing issues such as allowances for bad debts. The BADC is therefore the main source of auditing standards in Japan. The first set of auditing standards was issued in 1950, following the enactment in 1948 of the Securities and Exchange Law and the present CPA Law. They were subsequently revised in 1956 and 1965–6.

The auditing standards are in effect compulsory for all CPAs and audit corporations. The Ministry of Finance has issued a regulation which states that the audit of financial statements for Securities and Exchange Law purposes must be conducted in accordance with generally-recognised auditing practices, which shall be taken as meaning the auditing standards and working rules issued by the BADC (AICPA, 1975). The Ministry of Finance has therefore delegated the standard-setting responsibility to the BADC, whose auditing standards then have legal authority. Serious breaches of the standards would result in the CPA's licence being revoked by the Ministry of Finance. In some cases the CPA's licence could be suspended for a number of years, but this loss of prestige would end the CPA's auditing career, and consequently a suspension is effectively the same as the revocation of a licence. There is no enforcement procedure for

monitoring compliance with the standards, and the disciplinary procedure is rarely invoked unless breaches of the
standards come to light following a corporate collapse.

7.3   AUDITING STANDARDS – SCOPE AND CONTENT

From a Western perspective, the independent audit is
generally of more significance than the statutory audit under
the commercial code. The independent audit under the
Securities and Exchange Law corresponds more closely to
the Western concept of an audit, and is applied only to
publicly-traded (that is, relatively significant) companies.
The function of the statutory auditor is not comparable to
that of either an internal or an independent auditor
(AICPA, 1975). Consequently, this section concentrates on
the auditing standards governing the independent audit.

First, however, a few details are provided of the auditing
standards relating to statutory audits under the commercial
code. The statutory auditor is governed by relatively few
codified auditing standards. Certain reporting requirements
are contained in a 1974 law, namely the 'Law for special
measures under the commercial code with respect to
auditing, etc. of a stock corporation'. This law requires the
statutory auditor of a large company (capitalised at over one
billion yen) to report on the content of the business report,
improper acts of the directors, reasons why a proper audit
could not be performed (if that were the case) and the
reasonableness of the independent auditor's examination
methods. There are certain amendments for smaller companies.

Independent audits under the Securities and Exchange
Law are governed by the codified auditing standards issued
by the BADC (JICPA, 1974). The scope of these auditing
standards is therefore restricted to the independent audits of

the financial statements of the 2800 or so Japanese companies which are publicly traded. In practice, these auditing standards are usually also complied with by those CPAs and audit corporations who perform independent audits on large non-public companies (as described earlier).

The codified auditing standards include sections on auditing standards, working rules of field-work and working rules of reporting. The first section is phrased in general terms whereas the other two sections are more specific. All three sections must be complied with, although the second section permits a degree of flexibility (as discussed below).

The section on auditing standards contains three subsections, namely general standards, standards of field-work and standards of reporting. The first general standard states that the auditor should have adequate professional ability and practical experience as an auditor. Also, the auditor should have no material relationships with his clients. This is an unusual combination of an 'education and training' standard with an 'independence' standard. The second general standard requires the auditor to maintain an independent attitude when collecting data, exercising judgement and expressing his opinion. The third general standard requires the auditor to exercise due professional care in performing his examination and preparing his report. The fourth general standard requires confidentiality and forbids insider dealing.

The first standard of field-work requires that the auditor should perform an examination timely and systematically, based on an appropriate audit programme. Assistants, if any, should be subject to adequate instruction and supervision, based on an appropriate programme. The second standard of field-work states that the auditor should determine rationally the extent of his audit tests, based on his evaluation of the internal controls and the degree of his reliance thereon. The third standard of field-work requires the auditor to perform an examination with adequate consideration to materiality, relative risk and other elements inherent in the items to be examined, up to the point where his examination provides him with a reasonable basis for the expression of an opinion on the financial statements.

The first of the three standards of reporting says that the auditor should state clearly in his report the scope of his audit work and his opinion on the financial statements. The second reporting standard says that the auditor should state his opinion on whether the financial statements present fairly the enterprise's financial position and results of operations. The third reporting standard requires the auditor to disclose items which may not affect the financial statements being reported on but which may have a material affect on future financial statements.

The next section in the codified auditing standards is titled 'Working rules of field-work' and consists of detailed auditing procedures. A distinction is made between 'customary auditing procedures' and 'other auditing procedures'. Customary auditing procedures are defined as 'those customarily employed by the auditor in his examination of the financial statements' and they should not be omitted whenever practicable and reasonable (JICPA, 1974). The phrase 'whenever practicable and reasonable' seems to allow the auditor scope for judgement in the extent to which he needs to apply these procedures. Other auditing procedures are defined as 'those which should be employed in addition to the customary auditing procedures when the auditor considers them necessary under the circumstances' (JICPA, 1974). The working rules of field-work are all classified as 'customary auditing procedures', and hence the 'other auditing procedures' are uncodified. Customary auditing procedures are described under three main headings, namely auditing procedures for preliminary review, auditing procedures for records of transactions and auditing procedures for financial statements items. Auditing procedures for records of transactions are basically compliance tests, designed to ascertain whether the internal control system is operating effectively and whether the company's transactions are being recorded in accordance with the BADC accounting standards. Auditing procedures for financial statements items are basically substantive tests. The purpose of these tests is first to ascertain the 'propriety' of the account balances and the method of disclosure, and secondly to ascertain whether the financial statements comply with the BADC accounting standards and present fairly the company's financial position and results of operations.

The final section of the codified auditing standards is titled 'Working Rules of Reporting'. This is relatively brief (less than two pages, compared to fourteen pages in the previous section). The working rules of reporting say that the auditor should disclose the following in his report:

- Description of financial statements examined
- Whether the auditing standards were complied with
- When any significant 'customary auditing procedures' were omitted, a note of that fact and the reasons therefor
- Whether the financial statements fairly present the financial position and results of operations, by referring to conformity with BADC accounting standards, consistency of accounting principles, and compliance with regulatory requirements; and by referring to important exceptions to these
- (If applicable) his opinion that the financial statements do *not* fairly present the financial position and results of operations, and the reasons therefor
- (If applicable) that he disclaims an opinion on the financial statements, and the reasons therefor
- Events having a material effect on subsequent financial statements

7.4 SUMMARY

The Japanese auditing and accounting environment is

dominated by government influences rather than by the accounting profession. Nevertheless, Japan has an impressive list of codified auditing standards. As with other countries, the extent of compliance with these standards is difficult to determine. A survey of Japanese financial reports (Campbell, 1983) indicated a high level of compliance with *accounting* standards and requirements, and this may provide some insight into national attitudes towards complying with rules. However, an assessment of compliance has to be viewed against a background of a relatively new and undeveloped auditing profession.

8 The Netherlands

8.1 THE AUDITING AND ACCOUNTING ENVIRONMENT

The financial reporting environment in the Netherlands is influenced by a unique mix of public and private sector sources. Although the present reporting rules and recommendations are of relatively recent origin, Dutch accounting has traditionally been held in high regard throughout the world. In general, the financial reporting environment in the Netherlands resembles that of the UK more than it resembles that of other Continental countries such as France, Germany or Italy.

In recent years the main legal influence on financial reporting has been the 1970 Act on Annual Accounts of Enterprises, which came into force in 1971 and was incorporated into the civil code in 1976. The EEC Fourth Directive was incorporated into Dutch company law in a 1983 Act that affects annual accounts covering periods starting on or after 1 January 1984. The 1970 Act has been translated into English by the Dutch accountancy body (*NIVRA, 1972*). Up until 1971, there were very few legal requirements governing the form and content of financial statements (Beeny and Chastney, 1978). However, the absence until 1971 of a statutory reporting framework did not seem to affect the quality of financial reporting, which was generally considered to be of a high standard. Indeed, Flint (1983) implies that the absence of a statutory framework was a significant contributing factor to the

93

development of high quality financial reports. This was because Dutch accountants were able to concentrate on reporting the underlying economic reality rather than devoting their energies to ensuring strict compliance with a detailed set of legal requirements.

The 1970 Act on Annual Accounts states the general objectives of financial reporting and provides a number of specific disclosure rules. The objectives of financial reporting were deliberately framed in general terms in order to permit a high degree of flexibility (Klaassen, 1980). Although there are no specific rules on asset valuation or income measurement, Section 5 of the Act requires companies to use valuation and measurement bases that comply with standards that are regarded as being acceptable in the business environment.

In order to clarify what standards were 'acceptable in the business environment', a private sector committee was formed in 1971 at the invitation of the government. This committee is known as the Tripartite Accounting Standards Committee (TASC), and is composed of representatives from the employers' associations, the trade unions, and the professional accountancy body. The committee's task is perceived by its chairman as being 'one of reviewing the accounting principles applied in practice and giving its opinion on their acceptability within the framework of the Act on Annual Accounts' (Schoonderbeek, in Schoonderbeek *et al.*, 1980). The TASC chairman goes on to say that although the TASC pronouncements are meant to influence practice, they are not mandatory. According to Schoonderbeek (1980), the TASC pronouncements 'can best be described as the authoritative opinions of an influential private group'. The TASC's implicit intention is that, by involving the business community and the auditing profession directly in the standard-setting process, the pronouncements will be phrased in such a way as to result in first, compliance by the preparers of accounts, and secondly, audit qualifications in the case of non-compliance. The TASC's statements were initially issued as 'considerations', but these have recently been reclassified as 'accounting guidelines' (TASC, 1981). This change in emphasis was reinforced by the TASC's decision to distinguish between those guidelines which are 'firm pronouncements' and those which are merely 'recommendations and observations'. Although the guidelines are not mandatory, the TASC hopes that the 'firm pronouncements' will be applied in all annual accounts *as if* they were binding in character. The guidelines were issued in 1981 in draft form only, with the intention of establishing definitive guidelines at a later date.

An important feature of the Dutch financial reporting environment is the Enterprise Chamber, which was set up by the 1970 Act as a special section of the Court of Justice in Amsterdam (Klaassen, 1980). Interested parties can bring a case to the Enterprise Chamber if they consider that a company's financial statements do not comply with the 1970 Act. The Chamber reaches a decision on whether or not it agrees with the plaintiff's case, and then states whether (and to what extent) the company's financial statements should be corrected. The case is heard in private, with the company's auditor acting as a key witness. However, much of the background information is made public when the Enterprise Chamber states its verdict.

The Enterprise Chamber is a powerful body, in that it has legal authority and can require companies to amend their accounting practices. Despite this, it has little direct impact on the standard-setting process, as its scope is limited to pronouncing on the particular cases which are laid before it. However, the Enterprise Chamber has a strong indirect influence on the financial reporting environment. This is because companies (and their auditors) appreciate that non-compliance with the law may result in bad publicity arising from an unfavourable verdict. The TASC's lack of authority is emphasised by the fact that the Enterprise

Chamber has made some decisions which seem to conflict with the TASC's pronouncements (Beeny and Chastney, 1978).

The legal influence on the auditing environment is found mainly in the company law requirement for all public limited companies and large private limited companies to appoint a *registeraccountant* to audit their annual accounts (ICAEW, 1976a). In certain circumstances subsidiary companies are exempt from this requirement. The law requires the auditor to examine the financial statements and to report thereon to the shareholders. The purpose of the audit is to confirm that the financial statements give a true and fair view of the company's financial position and performance. If the financial statements do not comply with the relevant legal provisions, then the audit report must state the extent of non-compliance (Sanders, 1977).

The Dutch accounting profession has traditionally had a strong influence on financial reporting practices. The main professional body, the *Nederlands Instituut van Register-accountants (NIVRA)*, was formed in 1967, but *NIVRA* was preceded by a number of professional bodies which can be traced back to 1883 (Flint, 1983). The Dutch accounting profession is largely self-regulatory, but operates within a broad framework of government regulation contained in the 1962 Act on the *registeraccountants* (which came into force in 1968). The Dutch accounting profession is considered to have an excellent international reputation (Stamp and Moonitz, 1978; Nobes and Parker, 1981).

NIVRA is not directly responsible for issuing accounting requirements or recommendations. It influences financial reporting through its membership of TASC (described earlier). It also influences financial reporting by establishing and maintaining high standards of education and integrity among its members (who are in general the only persons qualified to audit public companies or large private companies). These high standards are likely to influence the quality of Dutch auditing and the quality of the financial statements being audited.

The official stock exchange is situated in Amsterdam and is the oldest in Europe (Beeny and Chastney, 1978). More than half of the turnover on the stock exchange is attributed to dealings in the five major Dutch multinationals. Although the stock exchange has detailed rules concerning the admission of securities for quotation, it has no direct influence on the annual financial statements of Dutch companies.

8.2   AUDITING STANDARDS – SOURCE, HISTORY AND AUTHORITY

There is no formal set of auditing standards in the Netherlands. However, the Dutch professional body has published a number of pronouncements, some of which carry a significant degree of authority and can be equated to the type of codified auditing standards found in the UK or the US.

The main source of these pronouncements is *NIVRA's* set of 'Rules of Conduct and Professional Practice'. These rules were approved by the members of *NIVRA* in 1973 and were subsequently approved by the Minister for Economic Affairs. An English translation was published in 1977 (*NIVRA*, 1977). These rules deal with professional ethics and with standards of reporting. They are divided into three main sections. One section applies to all *registeraccountants*, one applies to those *registeraccountants* acting as auditors, and one applies to *registeraccountants* acting as public accountants. In practice, all three sections apply to a *registeraccountant* who gives an audit opinion on the annual accounts of a public limited company or a large private limited company. Non-compliance with the rules could result in the *registeraccountant* appearing before the disci-

plinary board, which is independent of *NIVRA*. The
disciplinary board *(Raad van Tucht)* consists of a judge from
a civil or criminal court and four *registeraccountants*. All five
are appointed by the members of *NIVRA* in general
meeting (ICAEW, 1978). There is a board of appeal *(Raad
van Beroep),* consisting of three judges appointed by the
Minister of Justice and two *registeraccountants* appointed by
the members of *NIVRA* in general meeting. Serious cases of
non-compliance with the rules could result in expulsion from
the professional body. Klaassen (1980) notes the long
history of *NIVRA's* disciplinary function and concludes that
this has been a much more important disciplinary mechanism than lawsuits based on the civil code. There are
therefore significant professional sanctions that can be
invoked in cases of non-compliance with these rules. Legal
sanctions can also be invoked under the 1962 Act, as the
Minister for Economic Affairs' approval means that the
rules have the force of law. However, there are no direct
enforcement or monitoring procedures.

Other auditing statements issued by *NIVRA* consist of
'Opinions' *(Meningsuitingen)* and 'Interpretations' *(Inter-
pretaties).* These have less authority than the 'Rules of
Conduct and Professional Practice'. However, these guidelines play an important part in the self-regulatory framework, because *NIVRA* considers that its members should
not deviate from these guidelines unless they can properly
justify such a departure.

NIVRA also publishes a number of other documents
which may influence the way in which Dutch auditors
perform their work. These publications have no formal
authority. Some of these documents are issued as 'Study and
Discussion Memoranda' *(Studierapporten en Discussie-
rapporten),* published by various committees of *NIVRA* to
inform its members and to stimulate professional discussion.
NIVRA also reproduces the auditing statements issued by
the two supranational bodies, IFAC and *UEC* (see Chapter

13). On the first page of each such reprint *NIVRA* comments on how that statement relates to the current Dutch situation. These comments specify the extent to which the IFAC or *UEC* statement is, or will or will not be, incorporated into a Dutch Opinion or Recommendation or Study and Discussion Memorandum.

8.3 AUDITING STANDARDS – SCOPE AND CONTENT

The previous section explained that, although the Netherlands has no formal set of codified auditing standards, there are various rules and guidelines which influence the Dutch auditor's work. In general, these rules and guidelines apply to all situations where a *registeraccountant* expresses an opinion on the truth and fairness of a company's financial statements. This section describes the content of these rules and guidelines.

The main source of auditing rules is *NIVRA's* 'Rules of Conduct and Professional Practice' (section references below refer to these rules). The key elements of these rules can be classified into the following groups, which are described in detail below.

- Independence
- Confidentiality
- Due care
- Reporting
- Other auditors
- Documentation
- Offer of services

The independence rules are contained in section 9 and sections 22 and 23. Section 9 says that a *registeraccountant* shall be impartial in forming his opinion. Section 22 says that a *registeraccountant* must be independent of the person or legal entity that appointed him or on whose affairs he gives a report. A *registeraccountant* would not be independent of a client if he relies on that particular client for a continuous and material part of his income. Stamp and Moonitz (1978) say that these independence rules are interpreted as preventing Dutch accountants from doing tax or management consultancy work. However, this is not the case. The correct interpretation of the independence rules is given in an ICAEW publication (1978), which states that *register-accountants can* perform tax and consultancy work. The ICAEW publication also says that a *registeraccountant* may carry out a reporting function and an advisory function on the same client, provided that the *registeraccountant* exercises impartiality and independence towards his client in both functions.

The confidentiality rules are contained in section 10, which says that a *registeraccountant* acting as auditor must not make any use of confidential information beyond what is required for the discharge of his duties. This prohibits insider dealing as well as prohibiting unnecessary disclosure of confidential information. Section 10 is therefore more rigorous than the Dutch civil code, which forbids the auditor from disclosing more about the company's affairs than his duty as auditor requires (ICAEW, 1978).

Rules on due care are contained in section 11, which states that 'A *registeraccountant* shall make no statement on the outcome of his activities unless his expert knowledge and the work done by him provide a sound basis for his statement' (*NIVRA, 1977*). The *registeraccountant* must ensure that any such statement clearly reflects the outcome of his activities.

The largest group of sections of the rules of conduct deals with reporting. Section 12 states that the tenor of a *registeraccountant's* report should come within one of the following three categories:

● Approving, with or without a qualification

- Disapproving
- Withholding an opinion

An approving report implies that the *registeraccountant* has formed the opinion that the annual accounts give such insight into the company's financial position and results as is required under the circumstances. *NIVRA* has recommended the following wording for an unqualified report:

> We have examined the annual accounts of . . . for the year . . . In our opinion the annual accounts give a true and fair view of the size and composition of the company's capital and reserves as at . . . and of the size and composition of its results.

A *registeraccountant* should give a qualified approving report when there exist objections or uncertainties that, although not materially affecting the approving tenor of the report, are of such significance that they should be disclosed in the report (section 13). The words 'subject to' should be used in a qualified approving report (section 14).

A *registeraccountant* should give a disapproving report when he has formed the opinion that the accounts do not comply with the relevant requirements (section 13). The words 'not a true and fair view' or 'incorrect' should be used, and the nature and significance of the objections should be disclosed (section 14).

A *registeraccountant* should give a report withholding an opinion when he is faced with such uncertainties that he cannot approve or disapprove the fairness of the accounts taken as a whole (section 13). The report should describe the matters in respect of which the uncertainty exists (section 14).

Sections 15 and 16 include certain rules regarding the use of the opinion of another auditor or specialist (including the use of the opinion of an internal auditor). Sections 29 to 31 include certain rules of professional etiquette that should be followed when there are changes in professional appointments.

Rules on documentation are contained in section 18, which requires a *registeraccountant* to record his activities in such a way that a proper representation of his activities can be derived from these records. He must keep these records for at least ten years.

Section 28 states that a *registeraccountant* must not offer his services without having been invited to do so and he must not advertise.

The main components of *NIVRA's* rules of conduct and professional practice are therefore the ethical standards and the reporting standards. There are also field-work standards such as due care and documentation.

Standards of education and training are incorporated into the requirements for qualification as a *registeraccountant* (ICAEW, 1977). The entrance requirements to the Dutch accounting profession are rigorous and students do not normally qualify as *registeraccountants* until they reach their early thirties.

NIVRA 'Opinions' and 'Interpretations' are less authoritative than the 'Rules of Conduct and Professional Practice'. However, they are still an important influence on the Dutch auditor. To date, *NIVRA* have issued five Opinions and seven Interpretations. The five Opinions deal with the following topics:

- The nature of the auditor's opinion on the financial statements of companies with going concern problems
- Quality control in auditing
- Post balance sheet events, dating of the audit report, and management representations
- Documentation of audit work performed
- Audit reports of financial statements in cases of uncertainty

The seven Interpretations deal with the following topics:

- Audit engagement proposals
- The care that a public accountant must take in connection with the publishing of his statement for the business register
- The interpretation of the words 'separate document' in section 6
- The role of the *registeraccountant* as an accountant employed by an economic entity
- Limits of acceptable publicity for a public accountant
- Public accountants and tax advisors acting in the name of a company
- Requests and provisions of information in connection with changes in professional appointments (Sections 29 and 30)

8.4 SUMMARY

The Dutch auditing profession is almost entirely self-regulatory, within a broad framework installed and directed by law. The professional body has issued certain rules and recommendations, but the Dutch auditor is to a large extent personally responsible for determining the conduct of the audit. Dutch society seems willing to allow this significant element of personal responsibility, and seems to recognise that the *registeraccountant's* professional skill and judgement is of a high standard. This skill and judgement is the product of a long and rigorous period of education and training.

9 The United Kingdom

9.1 THE AUDITING AND ACCOUNTING ENVIRONMENT

The UK has a long and respected history of auditing and accounting. Legal requirements for audited accounts (balance sheet only) date back to the Joint Stock Companies Act of 1844. UK accounting practices and UK accountants have had a significant influence on the development of financial reporting practices in many other countries.

The main factors which affect the UK auditing and accounting environment are company law, the accounting profession and, to a lesser extent, the Stock Exchange. The interaction between the first two factors has changed significantly in the 1980s following the incorporation of the EEC Fourth Directive into UK company law via the Companies Act 1981. Prior to this, financial statements were governed by a legal framework that laid down the general objectives of financial reporting and required certain specific disclosures. Within these general constraints, companies were permitted a high degree of flexibility in choosing accounting measurement and disclosure practices. The accounting profession was influential in the operation of this self-regulatory system, in that the professional bodies issued accounting requirements that attempted to standardise the main areas of difference. The Companies Act 1981 changed this by introducing a set of prescriptive measurement and disclosure rules that is far more detailed than the previous set. This brief summary provides the background against which to view the subsequent detailed comments on the different factors affecting the UK financial reporting environment.

Legal influences on the accounting environment are found in the Companies Act of 1948, 1967, 1976, 1980 and 1981. The 1981 Act substantially amended the 1948 Act, and the main legal requirements are in the new Schedule 8 of the 1948 Act. The need for accounts to show a true and fair view remains the over-riding requirement of financial reporting. However, the detailed rules in the various Acts must normally be complied with. If compliance with these rules will not result in the accounts showing a true and fair view, then additional information must be provided. Departures from the detail rules are only permitted where a true and fair view would not be shown even if extra information was given in addition to complying with the detailed rules.

The new Schedule 8 rules include the fundamental accounting principles of going concern, consistency, prudence and accruals. Schedule 8 also includes standardised balance sheet and profit and loss account formats. Some headings in the formats must be used on the face of the balance sheet or profit and loss account, whereas the information required under other headings may be relegated to the notes to the accounts. Schedule 8 provides specific rules on asset valuation, grouped under two headings of 'Historical cost accounting rules' and 'Alternative accounting rules'. Schedule 8 also includes more detailed disclosure rules than previously existed.

Legal influences on the auditing environment arise from the Companies Acts and from case law. Company law requires that *every* company must appoint an auditor. In general, the auditor must be a member of the ICAEW, ICAS, ICAI or ACA. These four bodies are often referred to as the 'section 161 bodies', after the section in the Companies Act 1948 that sets out the qualification requirements for appointments as auditors.

The history of the accounting profession can be traced back to 1854, when a royal charter was granted to the Society of Accountants in Edinburgh. There are now six professional bodies in the UK and Ireland, as follows:

- The Institute of Chartered Accountants in England and Wales (ICAEW)
- The Institute of Chartered Accountants of Scotland (ICAS)
- The Institute of Chartered Accountants in Ireland (ICAI)
- The Association of Certified Accountants (ACA)
- The Institute of Cost and Management Accountants (ICMA)
- The Chartered Institute of Public Finance and Accountancy (CIPFA)

Members of the ICAEW, ICAS, ICAI and ACA normally work in private practice (as partners or employees of accounting firms) or in industry. Members of ICMA work almost exclusively in industry, whereas members of CIPFA work almost exclusively in local government accounting or auditing. There have been various moves to merge or restructure the professional bodies, but with little success to date. There are many formal and informal links between the councils (and the members) of the six bodies. All six bodies are represented on the Consultative Committee of Accountancy Bodies (CCAB), whose intention is to provide a focal point for outsiders wishing to deal with 'the' accounting profession. The Accounting Standards Committee (ASC) is a committee of CCAB, and is responsible for preparing Statements of Standard Accounting Practice (SSAPs). The SSAPs have to be approved by all the individual professional bodies, who then issue the SSAPs to their members. The SSAPs are intended to codify best accounting practice and to limit the range of treatments in any particular accounting issue.

The SSAPs are the main professional influence on the UK

108   *Comparative International Auditing*

financial reporting environment. A less obvious, but nevertheless significant, professional influence arises from the
high professional standards of qualified accountants, who
occupy many of the senior financial positions in industry and
consequently act as preparers of financial statements. One
of the objectives of the section 161 bodies' long and rigorous
education processes is to ensure that qualified accountants
will be aware of the limits beyond which financial statements
are no longer true and fair. The intention is that qualified
accountants will be able to accept or reject financial
reporting practices on the basis of uncodified professional
standards as well as by reference to the codified standards
represented by the SSAPs. Such an objective would have
less relevance in countries such as the United States where
relatively few senior financial positions are occupied by
members of the accounting profession.

The Stock Exchange requires listed companies to comply
with a number of financial reporting rules. These rules relate
mainly to disclosure rather than measurement aspects. For
example, a listed company must issue interim accounts
covering the first six months of its financial year. These
interim accounts must disclose certain specified items such
as sales, profit before tax and extraordinary items, and profit
attributable to shareholders. Annual reports of listed companies must include certain items, principally relating to
subsidiaries and to directors. The Stock Exchange's financial
reporting rules are noticeably fewer in number than those of
company law or the accounting profession. However, it
exerts a significant influence on the financial reporting of
listed companies, because material non-compliance with
company law or SSAPs may lead to varying degrees of
criticism from the Stock Exchange.

There is a well-developed financial press and community
of investment analysts in the UK. The financial press and
analysts frequently comment on good and bad examples of
measurement and disclosure practices, and this may have an

influence on companies wishing to attract good and avoid bad publicity. The financial press affects (and also reflects) public opinion of what are acceptable and desirable reporting practices.

9.2 AUDITING STANDARDS – SOURCE, HISTORY AND AUTHORITY

Codified auditing standards in the UK are referred to as Auditing Standards. The capital letters distinguish the codified Auditing Standards from uncodified auditing standards. The UK Auditing Standards are prepared by the Auditing Practices Committee (APC), a committee of the CCAB. The Auditing Standards have to be approved by all the relevant professional bodies, namely the ICAEW, ICAS, ICAI, ACA and CIPFA, who then issue the Auditing Standards to their members. The APC's role in establishing Auditing Standards is therefore similar to that of the ASC in establishing accounting standards. The APC's members are drawn from the above five bodies.

The history of the UK Auditing Standards must be placed in the context of the self-regulated nature of the UK auditing profession. In general, the government has accepted the integrity and standing of the auditing profession and has left the profession to produce its own rules and procedures. Company law sets out the auditor's duties, but it is left to the individual auditor (and to the profession) to determine how these duties should be fulfilled.

Until the 1970s, the profession relied mainly on uncodified standards of professional behaviour and conduct. In addition to these implicit standards, the professional bodies issued various auditing statements such as the English Institute's 'U' series (ICAEW, 1961–79) and the Scottish Institute's 'Series 3' (ICAS, 1971–7). These statements were recommendations rather than requirements. However, although there were no penalties for non-compliance with these specific statements, professional sanctions could be invoked in cases of serious professional misconduct, and the courts of law were available for any injured party who claimed that an auditor had been negligent.

In the mid-1970s the professional bodies decided to move towards the codification of auditing standards. This decision was influenced to a large extent by government pressures which arose subsequent to particular well-publicised instances of substandard accounting and auditing practices (Sherer and Kent, 1983). It could be argued that the auditing profession suddenly discovered the need to produce an approved set of auditing standards before the government intervened and did it instead. This interpretation is supported by reading between the lines of the introduction to the discussion drafts which preceded the final version of the codified Auditing Standards. Richard Wilkes, then chairman of the APC, commented in that introduction that the development of the codified Auditing Standards had a key role to play in convincing government and other audit report users that the profession was capable of adequate self-regulation (APC, 1978). The discussion drafts were issued in 1978, and the Auditing Standards (and related guidelines) in 1980. Several further guidelines have since been issued.

The authority of the Auditing Standards is indicated in the explanatory foreword issued with the standards and guidelines. Paragraph 11 of this explanatory foreword says that 'Apparent failure by members to observe Auditing Standards may be enquired into by the appropriate committees established by the Councils of the accountancy bodies, and disciplinary action may result'. This effectively means that the Auditing Standards are compulsory for members of the relevant bodies. Although an auditor could have ignored the recommendations in the previous professional auditing statements if he had proper justification, all auditors are now expected to observe the Auditing Standards. The

Auditing Guidelines provide guidance as to how the Auditing Standards may be applied, and do not have the same authority as the Standards. The Auditing Standards and Guidelines have no legal authority, but the explanatory foreword advises that the courts may take the Auditing Standards and Guidelines into account in determining good practice when considering the adequacy of a particular auditor's work.

The APC also issues Audit Briefs on particular topics. The Audit Briefs are indicative of current best practice in these areas but they do not have the same authority as the Auditing Standards or the Auditing Guidelines. The APC also issues a periodical entitled *True and Fair,* which publicises the work of the APC and comments on topical auditing issues.

The Auditing Standards do not refer to enforcement procedures. This is the responsibility of the individual section 161 bodies. To give an example of how these bodies discharge their responsibility, the Scottish Institute's Audit Practices Committee (not to be confused with the CCAB's Auditing Practices Committee) has considered three possible options:

- Go and look at audit work on a random basis
- Go and look at audit work only when suspicions are aroused
- Await complaints

Having assessed these options against the criteria of feasibility, cost-benefit for the public and effect on the profession's public image, the committee concluded that the Institute should adopt the third option (*The Accountant's Magazine,* 1980a).

The Joint Disciplinary Scheme (JDS) is an important element of the enforcement process. The JDS was set up at the end of 1979 by the ICAEW, ICAS and ACA, with the objective of maintaining proper standards of work and behaviour by the members of the three participating bodies. Consequently, the scope of the JDS includes not only auditing but also accounting, tax and management consulting services. The participating bodies would be entitled to refer serious departures from the Auditing Standards to the Executive Committee of the JDS, who would then appoint a Committee of Inquiry. Adverse findings of the Committee of Inquiry are subject to an appeal to an Appeal Committee. In the case of an adverse finding against a member, the Committee of Inquiry would submit a complaint to the Disciplinary Committee of the relevant participating body. The Disciplinary Committee would then consider the Committee of Inquiry's findings and would impose the appropriate penalty. In the case of an adverse finding against a member firm (that is, a firm of public accountants in which members of the participating bodies are partners), the Committee of Inquiry has the authority under the JDS to impose the appropriate disciplinary measures.

9.3   AUDITING STANDARDS – SCOPE AND CONTENT

The UK Auditing Standards apply whenever an audit is carried out (unless the text of the standard indicates otherwise). The explanatory foreword defines an audit as 'the indpendent examination of, and expression of opinion on, the financial statements of an enterprise by an appointed auditor in pursuance of that appointment and in compliance with any relevant statutory obligation' (ICAS, 1980). Consequently, the Auditing Standards apply not only to statutory audits governed by the Companies Acts but also to any non-statutory audits performed by members of the five relevant professional bodies.

There are three Auditing Standards, one dealing with standards of field-work and two dealing with standards of reporting. The field-work standard is titled 'The Auditor's Operational Standard' and applies whenever an audit is carried out. The standard's five key paragraphs have the following headings:

- Planning, controlling and recording
- Accounting systems
- Audit evidence
- Internal controls
- Review of financial statements

These are also the headings of five Auditing Guidelines, which give general guidance on the procedures by which the Auditor's Operational Standard may be complied with.

The standard says that the auditor should adequately plan, control and record his work. Under the heading of 'Accounting systems', the standard says that the auditor should determine the system by which the enterprise records and processes its transactions. The auditor should then assess the adequacy of that system as a basis for the preparation of financial statements. The next paragraph says that the auditor must obtain sufficient audit evidence to enable him to draw reasonable conclusions therefrom. This evidence must be relevant and reliable. The next paragraph deals with internal controls. There is no obligation on the auditor to assess the enterprise's internal controls unless he wishes to place reliance on any of them, in which case he should ascertain and evaluate such controls. He should also perform compliance tests to determine whether these internal control procedures are being applied as prescribed. The last key paragraph of this standard requires the auditor to review the financial statements. This review, together with the conclusions reached from the other audit evidence obtained, must be sufficient to give the auditor a reasonable basis for his opinion on the financial statements.

The first of the two reporting standards is titled 'The

Audit Report'. This standard applies to the audits of financial statements that are intended to give a true and fair view of the state of affairs, profit or loss and, where applicable, source and application of funds. A future Auditing Standard will deal with the issues that arise when the auditor is reporting on financial statements that are not required to give a true and fair view. However, this future standard is still at an early stage of development.

The audit report standard says that the auditor's report should identify to whom it is addressed. The report should also identify the financial statements to which it relates. Paragraph 3 of the standard requires the auditor to refer expressly in his report to three items. First, he should state whether the financial statements have been audited in accordance with approved Auditing Standards. Secondly, he should refer to whether in his opinion the financial statements give a true and fair view of the state of affairs, profit or loss and, where applicable, source and application of funds. Thirdly, he should refer to any matters expressly prescribed by relevant legislation or other requirements.

The explanatory note to the standard gives an example of an unqualified audit report on the financial statements of a company incorporated in Great Britain. (Great Britain consists of the United Kingdom excluding Northern Ireland, where company law is slightly different). This is given below (amended to reflect the effects of the Companies Act 1981).

Auditor's report to the members of . . .

We have audited the financial statements on pages . . . to . . . in accordance with approved Auditing Standards.

In our opinion the financial statements (which have been prepared under the historical cost convention as modified by the revaluation of land and buildings) give a true and fair view of the state of the company's affairs at 31 December 19 . . . and of its profit and source and application of funds for the year then ended and comply with the Companies Acts 1948 to 1981.

The words in brackets are optional, and stem from paragraph 7 of the explanatory note. This paragraph says that the auditor should refer to the particular accounting convention used if he considers such reference necessary to avoid misunderstanding.

A subsequent Guideline entitled 'Auditors' Reports and SSAP 16 "Current Cost Accounting"' provides suggested wording to be used when reporting on current cost accounts. In most cases the current cost accounts are supplementary to the historical cost accounts (rather than being the main accounts), and are normally not intended to show a true and fair view (Skerratt and Tonkin, 1982). In such cases it recommends that the following 'compliance' paragraph should be included in the auditor's report on the historical cost financial statements:

> In our opinion the abridged supplementary current cost accounts set out on pages X to X have been properly prepared, in accordance with the policies and methods described in notes X to X, to give the information required by Statement of Standard Accounting Practice no. 16.

The other reporting standard is titled 'Qualifications in Audit Reports'. The scope of this standard is the same as for the audit report standard. It indicates when the auditor should qualify his report and standardises the forms of qualification that should be used. The auditor should qualify his report when he is unable to report affirmatively on the three items contained in paragraph 3 of the audit report standard (described above). The audit report may also need to refer to non-compliance with relevant legislation and other requirements. An audit qualification should refer to all material matters about which the auditor has reservations. The audit report should include all the reasons for the qualification, and should also include, if both relevant and practicable, a quantification of the effect of the qualification on the financial statements.

The standard divides types of qualifications into four forms, which should be used unless the auditor considers that to do so would not clearly convey his intended meaning. The particular form of qualification to be used depends on the nature of the circumstances giving rise to the qualification. These circumstances generally fall into one of two basic categories, namely uncertainty (preventing the auditor from forming an opinion on a particular matter), and disagreement (where the auditor *can* form an opinion on a matter but this conflicts with the views of the directors as expressed in the financial statements). Both these categories can be sub-divided into cases which are material but not fundamental, and cases which are fundamental. The forms of qualifications used in the different circumstances are as follows:

- Disclaimer of opinion (used for a fundamental uncertainty)
- Adverse opinion (used for a fundamental disagreement)
- 'Subject to' opinion (used for an uncertainty that is material but not fundamental)
- 'Except for' opinion (used for a disagreement that is material but not fundamental)

The first two forms of qualifications are clearly the most serious. In a disclaimer of opinion the auditor states that he is unable to form an opinion on whether the financial statements give a true and fair view. In an adverse opinion the auditor states that in his opinion the financial statements do not give a true and fair view. The two reporting standards are supported by a Guideline, 'Audit Report Examples', which gives examples of four unqualified audit reports and thirteen qualified audit reports.

It is interesting to note that the Auditing Standards do not deal with auditor independence nor with the education and training of the auditor. Paragraph 12 of the explanatory foreword refers to the personal standards that are described in the ethical guides of the professional bodies. For example, the English Institute's *Guide to Professional Ethics* (ICAEW, 1983) requires members to be independent and to maintain confidentiality. The concept of auditor independence in the UK is such that shareholdings by auditors in client companies are not permitted. However, there are no restrictions on the provision of tax advice and management consultancy services to audit clients. The professional bodies also have detailed requirements governing entrance to the profession, and issue recommendations relating to post-qualifying education.

As mentioned earlier, there are separate Auditing Guidelines on each of the five key paragraphs in The Auditor's Operational Standard, on auditors' reports and SSAP 16 and on audit report examples. There are also Guidelines with the following headings:

- Representations by management
- Events after the balance sheet date
- Amounts derived from the preceding financial statements
- Attendance at stocktaking
- Bank reports for audit purposes
- Building societies
- Charities

The APC has a number of projects in hand at various stages of development. These projects mostly relate to future Guidelines, although an Auditing Standard on audit reports (other than true and fair) should be issued in the future. However, at present this prospective standard is only in the stages of initial consideration by APC. Some of the Auditing Guideline projects are listed below, in approximate order of likelihood of publication (with those likely to be published soonest being listed first):

- Engagement letters
- Auditing in a computer environment
- Debenture trust deeds (part of an intended series on special reports of accountants)
- Trade unions and employers' associations
- Quality control
- Reliance on internal audit
- Financial information issued with audited financial statements
- Auditors' considerations in respect of going concern
- Housing associations
- Prospectuses and the reporting accountant
- Audit reports on banking and insurance companies

9.4 SUMMARY

The UK has a long tradition of a sophisticated and largely self-regulated financial reporting environment. However, government influences on accounting practices became significantly stronger with the incorporation of the EEC Fourth Directive into UK company law. The development of codified auditing standards was in many respects a reaction to the perceived threat of increased government intervention into the ways in which the auditing profession regulated the conduct of its members. The UK now has codified field-work standards and reporting standards, and there are also a number of persuasive but not prescriptive guidelines.

10 The United States

10.1 THE AUDITING AND ACCOUNTING ENVIRONMENT

The auditing and accounting environment in the United States is dominated by the Securities and Exchange Commission (SEC), the accounting profession and a private sector standard-setting body called the Financial Accounting Standards Board (FASB). The SEC is a government agency and represents the main government influence on financial reporting. There are no influential company laws dealing with financial reporting issues. The auditing and accounting environment is itself influenced by a number of legal and cultural factors.

US corporations are governed by the legislation of the particular state in which they are incorporated. These state laws regulate the internal administration of US corporations by prescribing the rights and duties of directors and shareholders. However, the state laws do not normally require the publication of audited financial statements (AICPA, 1975). The main source of government legislation affecting financial reporting is *federal* legislation, namely the Securities Act of 1933 and the Securities Exchange Act of 1934. These two Acts resulted from government and public concern following the stock market collapse in 1929 and the economic depression of the early 1930s. The unregulated nature of the securities market was considered by many to be a major factor contributing to the 1929 collapse and the subsequent depression (Benston, 1976).

The Securities Exchange Act of 1934 applies to all companies that are listed on recognised stock exchanges or that are above a certain size. The size criterion was amended in 1981 so that companies with over $3 million of assets and over 500 shareholders are now governed by the Act. The Act requires all companies within its scope to publish audited financial statements. Consequently, all listed companies and all large unlisted companies must produce audited financial statements. Conversely, there is no requirement for small privately-held companies to publish their financial statements.

The 1934 Act established the SEC to administer the two Securities Acts. The Act gives the SEC wide-ranging powers to promulgate measurement and disclosure rules to be followed by companies governed by the Act. The SEC has in general allowed accounting standards to be developed in the private sector (currently by the FASB) and has rarely exercised its standard-setting powers in this area. On the other hand, the SEC has established an integrated disclosure system, in which the financial statements are only a part of the 'basic information package'. The SEC expects companies to comply with the FASB standards when preparing financial statements to be filed with the SEC. There are close links between the SEC and both the accounting profession and FASB, and the SEC is committed to a policy of 'active oversight' of the private sector standard-setters (Mead, 1980). The SEC has issued a number of 'Financial Reporting Releases' (formerly 'Accounting Series Releases'), but these generally complement the requirements established by the private sector bodies. The latent power of the SEC in the standard-setting arena was demonstrated in 1978 when the SEC entered the controversial debate over oil and gas accounting and overruled part of the relevant FASB standard (Carsberg and Eastergard, 1981).

The general purpose of the SEC is to ensure full and fair disclosure to investors. The sanctions available to the SEC in enforcing compliance with its integrated disclosure system include the following (OECD, 1980):

- Administrative proceedings (including the requirement to amend disclosures or restate financial statements, and the possibility of delisting)
- Injunctive actions (also including the requirement to amend disclosures or restate financial statements, and the possibility of requiring changes in the board of directors)
- Criminal proceedings (referred to the Department of Justice)

The SEC has a large staff, and plays an active role in monitoring companies' financial statements. This monitoring mechanism is considerably more comprehensive than that performed by the Department of Trade and Industry in the UK. The SEC's role can best be summarised by saying that it is a powerful body which rarely has need to exercise its powers. The threat of government intervention seems to act as an effective stimulant for the private sector to work towards a satisfactory system of self-regulation.

Other than the SEC, the main source of government influence on the accounting environment is the US Congress itself. This influence is less apparent now than it was in the late 1970s, when two Congressional subcommittees issued reports that were highly critical of the accounting profession and of FASB (Zeff, 1979). These reports were normally referred to as the Moss Report and the Metcalf Report, after the two chairmen of the subcommittees. The Congressional investigations were considered to be instrumental in leading the AICPA to reconsider its self-regulatory mechanisms. This resulted in the creation of the AICPA's SEC Practice Section (discussed below). The threat of direct intervention by Congress receded in the early 1980s, largely because political attitudes to government regulation changed following the election of President Reagan in 1980.

The professional accounting body in the US is the

American Institute of Certified Public Accountants (AICPA), which can trace its history back to 1887. Membership of the professional body is voluntary, and a substantial number of certified public accountants (CPAs) do not join the AICPA. The licensing and regulation of CPAs is governed by state boards of public accountancy in each of the 50 states, the District of Columbia, the Virgin Islands and Puerto Rico (AICPA, 1975). The AICPA has been involved in setting accounting standards since 1936, initially through its Committee on Accounting Procedure. This committee was superseded in 1959 by a new AICPA body, the Accounting Principles Board. The standard-setting role was taken over in 1973 by FASB, which is independent of the AICPA. However, several members of FASB are CPAs, and the AICPA maintains close links with FASB's operations. The AICPA code of professional ethics requires its members to follow the accounting standards established by FASB (except in exceptional circumstances where to do so would result in the financial statements being misleading). The AICPA formed a new committee, the Accounting Standards Executive Committee (AcSEC), when the APB's standard-setting role was taken over by FASB (Zeff, 1979). AcSEC is the AICPA committee responsible for financial reporting matters, and has issued a number of Statements of Position (SOPs) on accounting issues. SOPs are persuasive, not mandatory. The AICPA publishes an annual survey of the financial statements of 600 large US companies under the heading of *Accounting Trends and Techniques,* and this is widely considered to be a major factor in improving the quality of US financial reporting (A. K. Mason, 1978).

An important feature of the AICPA is the self-regulatory procedure created in reaction to the Moss and Metcalf Reports. In 1977 the AICPA division for CPA firms was divided into two sections, namely the SEC Practice Section (SECPS) and the Private Companies Practice Section

(PCPS). These are monitored by an independent board called the Public Oversight Board. Both practice sections operate a system of peer review to monitor the quality control procedures of member firms. The SECPS has a Special Investigations Committee (SIC) which deals with cases of alleged audit failures. The SEC seems satisfied with the system of peer review but reserves judgement on the *in camera* nature of the SIC (Savage, 1983a). Olson (1980) has pointed out the problems caused by duplication in the system of self-regulation. The objectives of the AICPA self-regulatory programme are described in more detail in Larson (1983).

There are a number of factors in the US that lead to the AICPA being faced with greater difficulties than the UK Institutes in indirectly influencing corporate financial reporting. Senior financial positions in the US are far less likely to be occupied by professional accountants than in the UK, as the US has a greater tradition of educating financial managers via business schools rather than the accounting profession. Consequently, professional accountants are less likely to be directly involved in the preparation of financial statements in the US. Also, there tends to be no common professional background uniting the preparer and the auditor of financial statements. In practice, however, senior financial officers who do not have an accounting background generally rely on key assistants who *do* have such a background, and this may reduce the scale of the difficulties to some extent. A further factor is that, as mentioned earlier, many CPAs (particularly in private industry) do not belong to the AICPA. This means that the AICPA has no rights of enforcement over a substantial number of CPAs. However, as OECD (1980) points out, all the state boards of public accountancy have codes of professional ethics and generally require CPAs to comply with FASB pronouncements.

The FASB is the main standard-setting body in the US. Its

members represent a variety of interest groups, including preparers, auditors and users of financial information. FASB issues accounting standards in the form of Statements of Financial Accounting Standards (SFASs), of which over seventy have been issued to date. A lengthy consultation procedure takes place before a final standard is issued. This 'due process' of consultation and exposure is designed to attract a high level of participation in the standard-setting process by all interested parties. This participation in the production of the finished article is intended to lead to a greater degree of support for the published standard. FASB also issues interpretations of the SFASs. One of its major projects has been the attempt to develop a comprehensive conceptual framework for financial reporting.

The SFASs have substantial authority in determining corporate reporting practices, as both the SEC and AICPA expect the standards to be complied with. The SEC seems to have been generally satisfied with FASB's performance since the oil and gas controversy in 1978 (referred to above). However, the SEC has criticised FASB for making slower progress than had been expected (Savage, 1983a). Savage also refers to the opposite criticism from the accounting profession, that FASB is responsible for 'standards overload'. Despite these criticisms, it appears that FASB will maintain its authoritative standard-setting role for some years.

The various US stock exchanges play a significant part in the economic and business environment, but they have little direct influence on annual financial reporting practices. Their disclosure requirements concentrate instead on immediate disclosure by companies of significant events (Benston, 1976). Benston also points out that the geographical spread of the US stock exchanges makes it harder for the financial community to apply the sanction of ostracisation of undesirable individuals (unlike the UK, for example, where the financial community is concentrated almost exclusively in one square mile in London).

The litigious nature of the US society is another important feature of the financial reporting environment. The willingness to sue in the US is affected by a number of factors, such as class actions, whereby one of a number of injured parties fights a 'test case', which, if successful, leads to the other injured parties automatically being compensated. Other factors include the tendency of lawyers to be paid on a contingency basis, calculated as a percentage of damages awarded, and the defensive nature of the legal profession itself, in that lawyers perceive the need to sue on a widespread basis in case *they* are subsequently sued for negligence.

These factors combine to create a situation which discourages experimentation in financial reporting. Companies and their auditors may consider it safer to shape particular transactions to fit within the strict letter of the rule-book rather than to shape the manner of measuring and disclosing accounting information to fit the particular facts and circumstances.

10.2 AUDITING STANDARDS – SOURCE, HISTORY AND AUTHORITY

There are several types of auditing pronouncements in the US. The most important is the set of ten 'generally accepted auditing standards' promulgated by the AICPA (AICPA, 1983). These standards were adopted by the AICPA in 1948 and 1949 and have remained broadly similar since then. The authority of these standards is contained in one of the rules of conduct of the AICPA Code of Professional Ethics (AICPA, 1983). Rule 202 says that an AICPA member must comply with the generally accepted auditing standards. The Code of Professional Ethics derives *its* authority from the

AICPA bylaws, which provide that the disciplinary body (the Trial Board) may administer penalties such as admonishment, suspension or expulsion in cases where a member is found guilty of infringing any of the rules of conduct. The AICPA generally accepted auditing standards are therefore supported by a powerful array of sanctions.

The next level of auditing pronouncements is the series of Statements on Auditing Standards (SASs) issued by the AICPA's Auditing Standards Board (ASB). The SASs interpret the ten generally accepted auditing standards. The ASB is the AICPA's senior technical body designated to issue pronouncements on auditing matters. The AICPA's Auditing Standards Executive Committee (AudSEC) issued the SASs until 1978, when AudSEC was superseded by the ASB. The SASs replaced the series of Statements on Auditing Procedure (SAPs) in 1972, when the existing SAPs were codified into SAS 1. The authority of the SASs is also contained in Rule 202 of the AICPA Code of Professional Ethics. Rule 202 says that departure from the SASs must be justified by those who do not follow them. The authority of the SASs is therefore significantly different from that of the generally accepted auditing standards. The difference is that whereas AICPA members *must* comply with the generally accepted auditing standards, they need not comply with the SASs if they are prepared to justify such non-compliance. However, in practice it appears that it would be difficult to justify non-compliance with SASs, and so the effective authority of the SASs may in fact be similar to that of the generally accepted auditing standards.

The next level of auditing pronouncements are the series of Audit Guides issued by the relevant AICPA Committee and the series of Auditing Interpretations issued by the staff of the AICPA's Auditing Standards Division. The Audit Guides deal with specific industries or types of business and are considered to represent best practice in that particular audit area. The Auditing Interpretations are intended to provide timely guidance on the application of the ASB's pronouncements (such as the SASs). The Guides and Interpretations are reviewed by the ASB but they are not issued as authoritative ASB pronouncements. However, AICPA members may have to justify a departure from a Guide or Interpretation in cases where the quality of their work is questioned.

There is a series of Audit Guides that deal with specific industries or types of business. These are issued by the relevant AICPA Committee and are considered to represent best practice in that particular audit area. AICPA members may be called upon to justify departures from them.

The auditing pronouncements referred to above are all issued under the aegis of the AICPA. This begs the question of what auditing standards govern the work of those CPAs who do not belong to the AICPA. The answer is that those CPAs are subject to the requirements of the various state boards of accountancy, who would normally expect CPAs to comply with standards similar to those of the AICPA. It is likely that a court of law would take the AICPA pronouncements into account when determining the level of performance expected from a CPA.

10.3 AUDITING STANDARDS – SCOPE AND CONTENT

A member of the AICPA must comply with the generally accepted auditing standards whenever he permits his name to be associated with financial statements in such a way as to imply that he is acting as an independent public accountant (Rule 202 of the AICPA Code of Professional Ethics). This means that when an AICPA member signs (or intends to sign) any type of audit report on any type of financial statements, he must comply with the generally accepted auditing standards.

The standards comprise three general standards, three standards of field-work and four standards of reporting. The general standards deal with the auditor's personal qualities rather than with the way in which he performs and reports on his work. The first general standard says that the person or persons performing the examination of the financial statements must have adequate technical training and proficiency as an auditor. The relevant SAS notes the importance of the inter-relationship between the auditor's formal education and professional experience. The second general standard requires the auditor to maintain an independence in mental attitude. The relevant SAS says that the auditor must not only be independent, but must be *seen to be* independent. The third general standard requires the auditor to exercise due professional care in the performance of the examination and the preparation of the report. Due professional care is interpreted in the relevant SAS by quoting from a legal textbook, *Cooley on Torts*. This says that a professional who offers his service to another is understood as holding himself out to possess the degree of skill that is commonly possessed by others in that profession.

The first standard of field-work states that the work should be properly planned and that assistants, if any, should be properly supervised. The relevant SASs state that audit planning should involve the development of an overall strategy for the expected conduct and scope of the audit. Supervision includes procedures for instructing assistants, reviewing their work and dealing with differences of opinion that arise within the audit team. The second standard of field-work requires the auditor to carry out a proper study and evaluation of the internal control system, to provide a basis for relying on the internal controls in determining the nature, timing and extent of the audit tests to be performed. The relevant SAS indicates that a preliminary review of the internal control system should always be performed. However, the auditor would complete the study and evaluation of the system of internal controls only if he intended to rely on the system. The third standard of field-work requires the auditor to obtain sufficient competent audit evidence to give him a reasonable basis for forming an opinion on the financial statements. This audit evidence should be obtained through inspection, observation, inquiries and confirmation. This standard is supported by an SAS entitled 'Evidential Matter'. This deals with the nature, competence, sufficiency and evaluation of audit evidence. Some SASs deal with specific audit areas, namely receivables, inventories and long-term investments. Other SASs deal with topics such as client representations, materiality and audit risk, analytical review procedures and audit sampling.

The first standard of reporting requires the auditor's report to state whether the financial statements are presented in accordance with generally accepted accounting principles. The relevant SAS recognises that there is no single source of reference containing all such principles, but says that such sources include various FASB and AICPA pronouncements. A fair presentation requires that the accounting principles must be not only generally accepted but also appropriate in the circumstances, and that the financial statements must include all matters that may affect their use and interpretation. The second standard of reporting requires the auditor's report to state whether the accounting principles have been applied consistently. The relevant SAS says that accounting changes affecting consistency would include changes in accounting principles, changes in the reporting entity (excluding acquisitions and disposals of subsidiaries and branches) and corrections of errors in principle. The third standard of reporting states that the information disclosed in the financial statements is to be regarded as reasonably adequate unless otherwise stated in the auditor's report. The relevant SAS interprets this to apply to cases where management omits from the financial statements information that is required by generally accepted accounting principles. In such cases the SAS says that the auditor should provide the information in his report and take exception to the omission.

The fourth standard of reporting requires the auditor's report to contain either an expression of opinion on the financial statements or an assertion to the effect that an opinion cannot be expressed. If the auditor cannot reach an overall opinion on the financial statements, then he should state the reasons for this in his report. Whenever an auditor's name is associated with financial statements, the report should indicate clearly the character of the auditor's examination, if any, and the degree of responsibility he is taking. This last requirement seems to be designed to prevent misinterpretation in cases where the accountant is associated with, but does not audit, the financial statements. The relevant SAS provides examples of audit reports to be used in certain circumstances. The SAS gives the following example of an unqualified report on financial statements that include comparative figures for the preceding period.

> We have examined the balance sheets of ABC Company as of [at] December 31, 19X2 and 19X1, and the related statements of income, retained earnings, and changes in financial position for the years then ended. Our examinations were made in accordance with generally accepted auditing standards and, accordingly, included such tests of the accounting records and such other auditing procedures as we considered necessary in the circumstances.

> In our opinion, the financial statements referred to above present fairly the financial position of ABC Company as of [at] December 31, 19X2 and 19X1, and the results of its operations and the changes in its financial position for the years then ended, in conformity with generally accepted accounting principles applied on a consistent basis.

Departures from this unqualified opinion will arise in the following circumstances:

- The scope of the auditor's examination is limited in some way
- The auditor's opinion is based in part on another auditor's report
- A generally accepted accounting principle has not been complied with
- Accounting principles have not been applied consistently
- The financial statements are affected by material uncertainties
- The auditor wishes to emphasise a particular matter

Departures from the unqualified opinion fall into four categories. The two most serious categories are adverse opinions and disclaimers of opinion. An auditor should give an adverse opinion when he considers that the financial statements are not presented fairly in accordance with generally accepted accounting principles. A disclaimer of opinion should be used when there are such fundamental uncertainties or limitations in scope that the auditor considers that he cannot properly form an opinion on the financial statements. The other two categories are defined as qualified opinions. These should be used when the auditor considers that he cannot give an unqualified opinion but he has decided not to issue an adverse opinion or a disclaimer of opinion. A 'subject to' qualified opinion should be used when the qualification arises because of an uncertainty affecting the financial statements. An 'except for' qualified opinion should be used in all other cases. The four categories of departures from unqualified opinion correspond closely to the four categories in the UK.

The generally accepted auditing standards do not refer to standards of confidentiality. However, this is dealt with in Rule 301 of the AICPA code. Rule 301 states that a member of the AICPA must not disclose any confidential information obtained in the course of a professional engagement except with the consent of the client. This does not override the requirements of Rule 202 (auditing standards), nor does it prevent the member complying with a court order or an AICPA inquiry.

The AICPA are currently working on a number of auditing projects. No changes are planned to the ten generally accepted auditing standards, but certain existing SASs will be revised and some new SASs will be issued. The main auditing projects are as follows:

- Internal control in an EDP environment
- Analytical review procedures
- Audit of current value financial information
- Auditability and completeness
- Reporting on financial statements used in other countries

10.4 SUMMARY

Although a significant number of CPAs do not belong to the AICPA, the government and the public seem to have concluded that the AICPA is the most suitable body for issuing auditing standards. The ten generally accepted auditing standards have remained substantially unchanged for several decades, and have formed the model for codified auditing standards in a number of other countries. These ten standards are unlikely to change in the near future.

Part III
Other Issues in International Auditing

Part III

11 Transferring Domestic Auditing Standards Overseas

11.1 INTRODUCTION

This chapter discusses the issues raised by the need to audit an MNC's foreign subsidiaries. For ease of reference, the issues are examined from the perspective of the auditor of a UK MNC. However, the issues also apply to the audits of MNCs based in other countries.

In the UK, the need to audit foreign subsidiaries arises from the requirements of the Companies Acts (the Companies Act 1967, section 14 and the Companies Act 1948, section 150(i), as amended by the Companies Act 1976, section 8(i)). The legislation referred to states the requirements for the preparation and audit of group accounts.

The link with UK Auditing Standards is provided by paragraph 15 of the explanatory foreword to the Auditing Standards and Guidelines (ICAS, 1980). This says:

Application of Auditing Standards Overseas Auditing Standards may not be appropriate to the audit of financial statements prepared in overseas territories solely for local purposes where different requirements of law or of general practice prevail. Where, however, the overseas financial statements are to be incorporated into UK or Irish financial statements the audit of the overseas enterprise should conform to Auditing Standards in so far as this is necessary to ensure that the audit of the UK or

135

Irish financial statements as a whole is in accordance with Auditing Standards.

The purpose of this paragraph is to assure users of a UK MNC's financial statements that UK Auditing Standards have been applied to all parts of the MNC's operations, even though the results of some of these operations may have been audited by firms whose members do not belong to any of the section 161 bodies (and hence who are not themselves bound by UK Auditing Standards).

By definition, an MNC carries out a significant part of its operations overseas (through the medium of direct investment, that is to say through branches or subsidiaries set up abroad). The auditor of the MNC can audit these operations in one of three ways:

(1) An audit team can be sent from the UK to the overseas location for the duration of the audit;
(2) the overseas audit can be carried out by a member or associate firm of the same international auditing firm as the parent company auditor (if such an international arrangement exists); or
(3) a separate firm of auditors can be asked to carry out the overseas audit (on a 'sub-contracting' basis).

Although this chapter deals with problems which arise in all three cases, it should be noted that the first option is unlikely to be widely used, due to constraints on the resources (in terms of staff and expenses) needed to finance such a method, and also due to the difficulties arising from the lack of daily contact throughout the year with the overseas subsidiary. Also, the third option raises particular additional problems which are dealt with in the next chapter. These additional problems are considered separately as they have received a great deal of attention both within the professional bodies and within professional firms.

The remaining sections of this chapter deal with the major

problem areas, as follows. Section 11.2 describes the difficulties that arise from differences in language and in cultural environment. Section 11.3 deals with the differences in international perceptions of the audit function. Section 11.4 is concerned with international differences in generally accepted accounting principles. Section 11.5 analyses different concepts of independence and of education and training. Section 11.6 deals with problems of authority and enforcement. Finally, Section 11.7 provides a summary and conclusions. This chapter therefore sets out a framework of the major problems involved in transferring UK Auditing Standards overseas. Each component of this framework can be applied to a greater or lesser extent to any particular audit, depending on the circumstances of the auditing firm and of the MNC.

11.2 LANGUAGE AND CULTURAL BARRIERS

Perhaps the most obvious problem is the language problem. This may exist where the overseas subsidiary of the MNC is located in a country whose national language is not English. Communication problems may of course also exist where the overseas subsidiary of the MNC is located in a country whose national language *is* English. This is basically an extension of the communication problems encountered in uninational audits, and consequently is not discussed further here.

The language problem, as well as being the most obvious, is also one of the most important. In the audit of a large MNC, there may at times be daily communications passing between the parent company auditor and the auditors of the subsidiary companies. At the beginning of the audit, this is likely to include a detailed audit planning memorandum from the parent company auditor. This detailed audit plan is likely to refer to the UK Auditing Standards, and is also likely to include specific requirements with respect to audit objectives. As the audit progresses towards its final stages, the parent company auditor may send out requests for specific information. The overseas auditors will reply to these requests, and will usually themselves have queries to be answered by the parent company auditor. The communication process will normally culminate in a report submitted by each subsidiary company auditor to the parent company auditor. A large MNC audit will therefore have a complicated communications network, covering thirty or forty countries over the duration of the audit. Language problems may cause misinterpretations of requirements and of results, and this breakdown in the communications network may lead to a substandard audit. This explains why the quality of communication is of such importance in MNC audits.

Where the overseas subsidiary is located in a country whose national language is not English, then the extent of the language problem will depend on whether or not the subsidiary company auditor is a native English speaker. If the subsidiary company auditor is not a native English speaker, then he will have to communicate either in English, which is not his native tongue, or indirectly by way of translated instructions and replies. In either case there is a danger of misunderstanding. Nuances and shades of meaning may be lost, and 'jargon' terms and phrases may be misinterpreted. Therefore if the subsidiary company auditor is not a native English speaker, it seems essential for the parent company auditor to communicate in simple and clear language, avoiding the use of complex sentence constructions and words with specialised meanings. In order to reduce misunderstandings in communications *from* the subsidiary company auditor it would seem useful for the parent company auditor to restate such communications in slightly different terminology and then tell the subsidiary company auditor that this is what his communication was taken to mean. Alternatively, the parent company auditor could confirm the key points by telephone.

If, on the other hand, the subsidiary company auditor *is* a native English speaker, then the communication problem is substantially reduced. The problem is not of course removed altogether, as misunderstandings may still arise between two people speaking English as their first language. However, as stated earlier, such problems are not peculiar to MNC audits and hence will not be discussed further. Although the communication problem is substantially reduced when the subsidiary company auditor is a native English speaker, a 'lower-level' problem arises. This is because the subsidiary company auditor must communicate with his audit staff either in a language which is not his native tongue or by way of translations (if we assume that the audit staff are local nationals). This is not as serious a problem as that discussed in the previous paragraph, as presumably in this case such communications occur on a daily basis and both parties are likely to have more experience of dealing with the language problem.

In practice, one way that the Big Nine audit firms deal with the language problem within their own organisations is to instal a 'home' audit partner in the countries where their MNC clients have substantial interests. For example, the African or South American offices of the firm may include a resident UK partner, whose main responsibility is to deal with the audits of subsidiaries of UK companies rather than with the audits of purely local companies. This practice may also help to solve the other problems arising from the need to transfer auditing standards overseas.

Cultural barriers are more complex and less obvious than language barriers. Such cultural differences can be seen in the variety of legal, social, economic and political environments which exist throughout the world. Some of these cultural differences are expanded on in Sections 11.3 to 11.5.

Other effects of these environmental factors include different reactions to the notion of 'standards' of behaviour and performance. Compare for example the different reactions to upholding or breaking tax laws in certain countries. For obvious reasons, it is difficult to undertake research into the hypothesis that companies in some countries have two sets of accounting records – one for the owners, and one for the tax authorities. However, it seems reasonable to suggest that there may be international differences in attitudes to 'rule-breaking'. An additional problem is that in countries where the accounting profession is in its infancy, it is likely that no codified auditing standards will exist. In that case, the idea of auditing standards may be unfamiliar, and therefore local auditors may not appreciate the implications of the need to comply with standards in an auditing context.

11.3   DIFFERENT PERCEPTIONS OF AUDIT

The last section mentioned cross-cultural factors such as differing legal, social, economic and political environments. One impact of these differences is the range of variations in the objective of an audit. Differing perceptions of the audit function may lead to significant problems in transferring domestic auditing standards overseas. These problems arise because the parent company auditor's perception of the word 'audit' may differ materially from the perception of the auditor of the overseas subsidiary. For example, the subsidiary company auditor, on being asked to perform an 'audit', might perform an audit which is perfectly acceptable by his local standards. However, these local auditing standards may just require a check that the financial statements are in accordance with the bookkeeping records. This type of audit would not be as comprehensive as a UK 'true and fair' audit. In such a case, the subsidiary company auditor could report that he has completed an audit and the parent company auditor could wrongly assume that this is equivalent to a UK audit.

There are significant international differences in the nature of the audit function. For example, in Belgium company law requires the appointment of a statutory auditor *(commissaire aux comptes),* but his duties are limited to an overall review of the financial statements to ensure that they reflect the accounting books and records. (However, larger companies require an audit which corresponds more closely to the UK version.) (See ICAEW 1976b.) Similarly, in Switzerland the objective of an audit is to ensure that the financial statements are an accurate reflection of the company's accounting records (Arpan and Radebaugh, 1981). From a UK perspective, this seems to be a fairly 'lightweight' audit requirement, in that there is no need to check that the accounting records accurately reflect the underlying economic events, nor is there any need to ensure that the financial statements comply with the law or with standard accounting practice.

Another example is Germany, where the standard audit report refers to the fact that the financial statements 'comply with the law'. There could be cases where such compliance with the law could be perceived as being inconsistent with the presentation of a 'true and fair view', and in such cases the German auditor (unlike his UK counterpart) would treat legal compliance as the over-riding objective. It should be noted that this difference should be removed soon (within EEC member states) following implementation of the Fourth Directive, which says that the over-riding objective of financial statements is the provision of a true and fair view. However, this leads on to another problem, namely differing interpretations of 'true and fair view' (see Chastney, 1975). There is no agreed definition of this phrase in UK law, or in any UK accounting profession pronouncement. It is therefore not surprising that interpretations differ. A German auditor could argue that if the financial statements comply with the law then that is sufficient to ensure truth and fairness.

Having described some different perceptions of the audit function, it would seem useful to analyse why these international differences exist. The fundamental explanation is that the reasons for auditing outlined in Section 2.2 differ in importance from country to country. The AAA research study (1973) discussed in Section 2.2.3 argued that the demand for auditing arises from four factors: conflict of interest, consequence, complexity and remoteness. The relative importance of each factor may differ from country to country. The particular audit need which arises as a result of the mix of influences in one country may therefore differ from the audit need in another country.

For example, consider a country such as France, where companies have a history of ownership being restricted to a small number of shareholders (compared with the widespread ownership patterns and well-developed capital markets of the UK and the US). Consequently, there is little separation of ownership and control of the business, and hence conflict of interest does not present such a problem as in the UK or the US. For another example, consider Germany, where the banks have a history of direct investment in industrial enterprises (that is, they are providers of *share* capital as well as providers of *loan* capital as in the UK). In Germany, problems of remoteness are less important than in the UK, as the German banks presumably have relatively easy access to the subject-matter underlying the information contained in the financial statements. Problems of complexity are also of lesser importance in Germany, as the banks are likely to have suitably qualified and experienced personnel who are capable of judging the quality of the information processed and presented by the enterprise in question. These examples suggest that different structures of business organisations are a key factor in explaining different perceptions of the audit function.

Because differing perceptions of the audit function exist, the auditor of the UK MNC must ensure that auditors of the overseas subsidiaries understand the objective of a UK audit. This may involve familiarising the overseas auditor with the meaning of 'true and fair' in a UK context. Further differences in the perception of the auditing function are embodied in different attitudes towards personal standards such as audit independence and the education and training of auditors. These are discussed further in Section 11.5.

11.4   DIFFERENCES IN GENERALLY ACCEPTED ACCOUNTING PRINCIPLES

This chapter has already discussed how international differences in cultural influences can lead to different perceptions of the audit function. Such differences in cultural influences can also lead to different *accounting* environments. In this context the 'accounting environment' means the framework of requirements and recommendations governing the external financial reporting of limited companies. This section discusses the issues that different accounting environments raise for the auditor of a UK MNC.

The UK accounting environment is described in Chapter 9. The financial statements of a listed MNC are governed by measurement and disclosure requirements in the Companies Acts, statements from the professional accountancy bodies and The Stock Exchange Listing Agreement. There is an over-riding requirement for the financial statements to give a true and fair view of the MNC's state of affairs and balance sheet.

In the audit of a UK MNC, the parent company auditor will require auditors of overseas subsidiaries to report that the accounts package submitted to the UK for consolidation complies with the requirements of the UK accounting environment as outlined above. However, the overseas auditors may be operating in a very different accounting environment and hence may have little detailed knowledge of UK accounting requirements and practices. Richards (1976) discusses comparable problems arising in the audit of US MNCs.

An international comparison of accounting environments reveals many fundamental differences in accounting requirements and practices around the world. Descriptions and analyses of these differences can be found in AICPA (1975), Price Waterhouse International (1979) and Nobes and Parker (1981). Differences may occur where two countries have addressed the same problem but have arrived at different solutions or they may occur where one of the two countries has adopted a particular solution to an accounting issue and the other country has no generally accepted practice in that area. A few examples of international differences may help to illustrate the problems faced in MNC audits.

At present, the UK method of inflation accounting is based on current cost accounting. However, inflation accounting in countries such as Brazil and Chile is based on current purchasing power accounting. In the UK, tangible fixed assets such as land and buildings are often included in the financial statements at a valuation in excess of cost. This practice is not allowed in Germany, for example. In the UK, stocks are valued at the lower of cost and net realisable value, with cost normally being determined on a 'first-in, first-out' basis or a weighted average basis. However, in some countries (for example, the US) the 'last-in, first-out' basis is often used to determine cost.

A particular category of international differences occurs when the subsidiary is located in a country such as Zambia which has adopted *en bloc* the international accounting standards issued by the International Accounting Standards Committee. Differences arise when the UK accounting standard is more restrictive than the international accounting standard. Consider for example the topic of foreign currency translation, and in particular the accounting treatment of long-term monetary items denominated in a foreign currency. SSAP 20 (Foreign currency translation) states that exchange differences arising from the retranslation of long-term monetary items must be included in the profit and loss account for the year (except in certain circumstances where the 'cover' concept may be used, in which case exchange differences may be taken to reserves). However, IAS 21 (accounting for the effects of changes in foreign exchange rates) allows companies to *defer* exchange losses arising on retranslation of long-term monetary items (under certain conditions).

These few examples indicate the nature and extent of comparative international differences in accounting environments. The auditor of an overseas subsidiary of a UK MNC may be unfamiliar with particular aspects of UK accounting requirements and practice. The parent company auditor must therefore ensure that the overseas auditor is aware of the UK accounting scene and its developments.

One possible solution occurs when the MNC has a standardised accounting manual which is used in all its subsidiaries. If this accounting manual complies with all relevant UK accounting requirements, then the auditor of the overseas subsidiary simply needs to ensure compliance with this manual. Although such an accounting manual will tend to concentrate on *measurement* practices, it will usually also refer to standardised *disclosures* in the form of monthly/quarterly/annual reports. However, it should be noted that the wide range of differences in accounting practices throughout the world means that on occasion the requirements of the standardised accounting manual will differ from local requirements and practices. The most likely outcome in this case is probably a dual reporting system, where the accounts package (for consolidation in the MNC's financial statements) is prepared on one basis and another set of financial statements is prepared to meet local requirements.

A similar solution may occur in cases where there is no formal accounting manual but where the MNC issues detailed year-end reporting instructions to its overseas subsidiaries. If these reporting instructions are sufficiently comprehensive to include the MNC's accounting policies on all material measurement and disclosure issues, then the overseas auditor will normally be asked by the parent company auditor to report on compliance by the overseas subsidiary with these reporting instructions. This will reduce the need for the overseas auditor to learn about UK accounting principles from other sources.

International harmonisation of accounting standards would narrow the range of accounting practices adopted around the world, and would to that extent resolve the issues discussed in this section. However, although international harmonisation has occurred in some accounting topics, there are still areas of significant differences. Unless and until these are resolved, differences in accounting environments will continue to create significant problems in transferring auditing standards overseas.

11.5 DIFFERENT CONCEPTS OF INDEPENDENCE AND EDUCATION AND TRAINING

As was noted in Chapter 9, these topics are not included in the UK Auditing Standards, despite the initial optimism of the APC that such 'personal' standards would be included in its remit (see for example Auditing Practices Committee, 1976). The APC believes that personal standards are the responsibility of the section 161 bodies. Strictly speaking, therefore, the topics of independence and education and training should not be included in a discussion of the problems involved in transferring the UK Auditing Standards overseas. However, these topics deserve some attention because they form part of the *uncodified* auditing standards of the UK auditing profession, and hence the impact of any international differences in these standards needs to be considered by the auditor of the UK MNC. This need arises because the international user of the MNC's financial statements (assuming he is aware of the uncodified 'personal' standards applicable to the UK auditor) is entitled to assume that such standards have been met throughout the whole audit.

11.5.1 Independence

Although independence is not one of the matters dealt with in the UK Auditing Standards, it has been the subject of various pronouncements from the UK professional bodies (for example, ICAEW (1983)). The concept of auditor independence is normally considered to be one of the key components of the auditing environment. Lee (1972) points out the close relationship between user confidence in the accounting information and the position of independence adopted by the auditor. As the auditor's independence increases, so too does the probability of shareholders and others having confidence in his work and opinion. Firth (1980) supports this by referring to the traditional view of auditor independence, namely that lack of independence will reduce the importance placed on audit reports and that investment and loan decisions will be impaired. However, the results of Firth's research show that non-independence may create perceived benefits to the client in certain circumstances. Different countries give differing weights to the costs and benefits arising from particular auditor-client relationships, and hence international perceptions of independence may differ significantly.

One area of difference concerns whether or not the

auditor may be involved in direct financial relationships with his client. For example, at present statutory audits of small companies in countries such as Belgium, France and Switzerland may be carried out by shareholders. However, in the UK and the US such direct financial involvement is not permitted (and it is only fair to say that neither is it permitted for audits of *large* companies in the three above-mentioned countries). Another example arises in countries like Germany, where banks may hold a majority share of the equity ownership of auditing firms. Although such ownership is kept separate from the control over the policy-making of such firms, thus allowing claims of independence, it is clear that such arrangements would not pass the UK independence requirements.

Another area of difference concerns whether or not the auditor may provide other financial services to his client (for example, tax advice, accounting services, management consultancy work). In this area most Western European countries tend to take a harder line than the UK and the US. Some Western European countries argue that the auditor cannot hope to be perceived as being independent if he relies on his audit clients for fees for other services rendered (see for example Bartholomew, 1978; and Dykxhoorn and Sinning, 1981).

Although the UK and the US show a more relaxed attitude to the provision of non-audit services, the issue has still been the subject of some debate in these countries. For example, the Cohen Commission (AICPA, 1978) considered the issue and concluded that the provision of non-audit services does not seem to impair auditor independence. However, it also concluded that the *perception* of auditor independence is sometimes affected in such cases. Recent research into auditor independence has produced some interesting (and apparently conflicting) results. Firth (1980) examined perceptions of auditor independence in the UK, and found that in general the perceptions of practising

accountants were in line with the professional pronouncements on auditor independence. However, users of financial
statements were frequently more sceptical of auditor independence. This difference was particularly noticeable on the
question of auditing firms providing management consultancy services to their audit clients. In the US, research
carried out by Reckers and Stagliano (1981) showed that
both sophisticated and unsophisticated users of financial
statements expressed a high level of confidence in the
auditor's ability to remain independent while performing an
average level of non-audit services for clients. Other
research carried out in the US allowed Shockley (1981) to
reach the conclusion that the provision of non-audit services
may impair perceptions of audit independence.

Therefore comparative international aspects of the independence issue involve not only differing legal and professional requirements but also differing perceptions (by
auditors and users) of auditor independence.

11.5.2 Education and Training

Professional qualifications for entry into the auditing profession differ throughout the world in respect of varying
emphasis on the quantity of academic qualifications, professional accounting examinations and practical experience.
Stamp and Moonitz (1978) discuss differences in professional qualifications in nine countries with developed
accounting professions. Significant differences exist between
these countries, and it is likely that more fundamental
differences will exist between the UK and countries with less-
developed accounting professions. The problem for the
auditor of the UK MNC is therefore greatest in the case of
subsidiaries in these countries, where local standards of
education and training may be significantly below the UK
level. The best solution in such cases would seem to be to

find someone with a professional qualification from the UK or an advanced accounting nation to audit the subsidiary company.

The EEC's Eighth Directive deals with the independence of the auditor and his professional qualifications (see Bartholomew, 1978; and Radford, 1980). IFAC and *UEC* are also concerned with the possibility of harmonising these personal standards (see Sempier, 1979; and McDougall, 1979). The work of these three bodies is discussed in more detail in Chapter 13. The auditor's independence and his professional qualifications are a fundamental part of the audit process. The MNC auditor must therefore be aware of international differences in these areas and he must also ensure that the auditors of all subsidiary companies do not fall short of the standards which exist in the parent country.

11.6   PROBLEMS OF ENFORCEMENT

By way of background to this section it should be noted that enforcement of the UK Auditing Standards is the responsibility of the individual section 161 bodies rather than of the APC. At present such policing only takes place when complaints are made or when public interest is aroused (rather than, for example, by random investigations of audit files). This indicates that the UK professional auditing bodies consider that there is no need for direct enforcement of the UK Auditing Standards. There is an implicit assumption that the professional integrity of UK auditors can be relied upon to ensure compliance with the profession's codified standards.

However, the subject-matter of this section is not so much enforcement in the UK, but rather how the auditor of the UK MNC ensures that the auditor of the overseas subsidiary complies with the UK Auditing Standards. Although the enforcement problem exists in a purely UK group where domestic subsidiaries are audited by firms other than the parent company auditor, this enforcement problem is relatively simple, as the subsidiary company auditors are directly required to comply with the UK Auditing Standards (since the subsidiary company auditors are members of the UK auditing profession). The MNC audit creates a much more significant enforcement problem, as the parent company auditor can no longer rely on the subsidiary company auditors being subject to the sanctions of the UK professional bodies.

The overseas enforcement problem arises from a combination of two factors. First, the fact that a separate auditor has been asked to audit the overseas subsidiary implies that the parent company auditor considers himself unable to audit the subsidiary himself (for reasons of time, cost and remoteness). Secondly, the nature of auditing implies that the work done by the subsidiary company auditor is summarised by the subsidiary company auditor himself.

Hence there is a danger that the subsidiary company auditor may report that he has complied with UK Auditing Standards even when this is not the case (with such negligence being either deliberate or accidental). If this seems too harsh a viewpoint then the reader should remind himself of the well-publicised cases of 'audit failures' which were a motivating factor behind the drive to establish the UK Auditing Standards (see for example Woolf, 1979, p. 24). If such failures can occur in a profession which considers itself among the world leaders in auditing, then it is perhaps not too cynical to suggest that non-compliance with standards may happen in other countries too.

The above paragraphs outline the nature of the problem. The remainder of this section analyses possible solutions. If the subsidiary company is being audited in a country with a set of auditing standards on a par with those in the UK *and* if these standards are directly enforced by the local auditing profession (or by the state), then the scale of the problem is substantially reduced. However, this ideal solution is a rare occurrence. A 'second-best' solution might occur where the subsidiary company is being audited in a country with a set of auditing standards on a par with those in the UK, and where these auditing standards are enforced in the same manner as in the UK (that is, on a 'wait for complaints' basis). In that case the parent company auditor might consider that he can rely on the professional integrity of the overseas company auditor, in the knowledge that the overseas auditing profession can invoke sanctions for non-compliance with the local standards.

One solution to the enforcement problem is for the parent company auditor to inspect the subsidiary company's audit files, either by travelling to the overseas location or by having the files sent to the UK. However, apart from the time and expense involved, this may be interpreted as a blatant lack of trust and could lead to considerable ill-feeling (in particular where the subsidiary company is audited by a member of the same international auditing firm as the parent company). Another solution is for the parent company auditor to issue questionnaires to subsidiary company auditors. These questionnaires can be designed to include questions relating directly to the specific UK Auditing Standards, and may also include a wide range of supplementary questions seeking information on the work done in particular audit areas. However, the difficulty with either of the possible solutions mentioned in this paragraph is that the evidence provided by the subsidiary company auditor (either in the audit files or the questionnaires) might not actually represent work performed.

Therefore it seems that unless the parent company auditor chooses to re-perform the work of his subsidiary company counterpart, then he must depend to a large extent on trust. This trust can be based on his knowledge of the professional standards that exist in the other country and on his personal knowledge of the other auditor. The relationship between the two auditors is also influenced by the fact that the parent company auditor normally controls the ultimate sanction of replacing the subsidiary company auditor. The existence of this sanction is likely to increase the chances of the subsidiary company auditor complying with the UK Auditing Standards when requested to do so by the parent company auditor.

This section on the enforcement problem concludes by pointing out that the growing pressure for increased auditor accountability (as evidenced by the influences behind the development of the UK Auditing Standards) may eventually lead to a need for more direct and more obvious enforcement of the UK Auditing Standards. If this happens then the act of faith mentioned in the previous paragraph may not be sufficient for the auditor of the UK MNC to ensure that the overseas auditor complies with UK Auditing Standards.

11.7 SUMMARY

This chapter has discussed the main issues involved in applying the UK Auditing Standards to the audit of an MNC's overseas subsidiaries. The discussion has been kept as general as possible in an attempt to construct a theoretical framework of the issues to be considered. The purpose of writing the chapter in general terms is that the more general the discussion the more widespread can be the application of the framework to particular cases. Had a more specific approach been adopted (for example, by concentrating on providing practical examples) then the application to any one particular audit might be limited.

The framework could be applied as necessary to the audit of the MNC in question, with the emphasis on the different elements of the framework depending on the inter-relationship between the circumstances of the MNC and of the auditing firm (in terms of international spread of operations). That is to say, the MNC auditor could identify the extent to which each section of the chapter applies to the audit in question, by analysing the geographical spread of the MNC's subsidiaries and the Auditing Standard transfer problems in each overseas location.

Finally, it should be emphasised that solutions have still to be reached for the problem areas outlined. Although one set of problems may be solved by issuing auditing standards as a codification of UK 'best practice', it should be apparent from the discussion in this chapter that significant problems still exist where an MNC's subsidiaries are located either in countries where best practice exists but has a significantly different meaning to that in the UK, or in countries where best practice does not exist in any meaningful sense at all.

12 Using the Work of Another Auditor

12.1 INTRODUCTION

Chapter 11 discussed the problems involved in transferring the UK Auditing Standards overseas. For the most part this discussion was framed in general terms without considering whether another firm of auditors was carrying out the overseas audit. However, in addition to the problems raised in Chapter 11, there are *further* problems which arise when another firm of auditors is used. These further problems are the subject of this chapter. This chapter therefore approaches the Auditing Standards transfer problem from a different angle to that used in Chapter 11. This chapter considers the issues involved in using the work of another auditor, concentrating on those areas that are highlighted when that auditor is overseas (that is, when the 'other auditor' is auditing an overseas subsidiary of the UK MNC). In this chapter the term 'primary auditor' is used to denote the auditor of the UK MNC (that is, the auditor responsible for the overall opinion on the group's financial statements). The term 'secondary auditor' is used to denote the 'other auditor' (that is, the auditor of the MNC's subsidiary).

The first task is to provide a more detailed definition of 'another auditor'. This is done in Section 12.2, which also discusses the implications behind alternative definitions. Section 12.3 deals with the problem of access to the other auditor's work. Section 12.4 discusses in general terms how the primary auditor should approach the problem of using the work of another auditor. Sections 12.5 and 12.6 deal with two specific problems, first, by discussing criticisms of the costs involved, and secondly, by discussing the problems that arise when different audit approaches are adopted. Section 12.7 provides a summary and conclusions.

12.2   DEFINITION OF 'ANOTHER AUDITOR'

If we consider the situation of a large UK MNC being audited in several locations within the UK and in several countries abroad, then it is apparent that a number of 'other auditors' are involved. The question to be answered is at what point on the scale does 'using another auditor's work' become an issue?

At one end of the scale there is (for example) the London-based auditor asking a partner in his firm's Birmingham office to audit the MNC's subsidiary there. A strict interpretation of 'auditor' as 'the person who signs the audit report and hence takes overall responsibility for the audit' recognises the uniqueness of personal identity and hence regards the Birmingham partner as 'another auditor'. However, it seems reasonable to assume that partners in a national firm subscribe to common auditing standards and procedures and hence the definition of 'auditor' should be widened to include partners in the same firm. This is the definition given in the UK Auditing Standards (ICAS, 1980), although there is no mention of whether 'firm' refers to national or international firm. However, as the Auditing Standards are approved by the section 161 bodies (that is, by the Uk auditing profession), then it seems reasonable to conclude that the national context is meant. Consequently, at this end of the scale we see that the issue of 'using the work of another auditor' does not arise when other offices of the same national firm are carrying out the audit. Quality control is still an issue, but it is not discussed here.

At the other end of the scale is the situation where the auditor who is a partner in the London office of one of the Big Nine auditing firms asks a Nairobi partner of another Big Nine firm to audit a Kenyan subsidiary. In such cases the secondary auditor cannot automatically be assumed to subscribe to the auditing standards and procedures of the primary auditor's firm, as there is no partnership agreement binding the two parties. Such a situation is clearly a case of 'using the work of another auditor'.

However, the situation becomes more complicated in the case where a London partner asks a partner in the Paris office of the same international auditing firm to carry out a subsidiary company audit. Can we assume that common auditing standards and procedures apply across the inter-national firm (as was assumed for the national firm in the first case above)? If so, it seems reasonable to suggest that the issue of 'using the work of another auditor' does not arise. Conversely, do we assume that the overseas firm's standards and procedures have developed in relation to the local accounting and business environment, and hence are not directly comparable with the UK firm's standards and procedures? If so, then the issue of 'using the work of another auditor' is likely to be of some importance.

The solution lies in recognising that the international auditing firms do not form a homogenous set. Weinstein *et al.* (1978) provide five models of organisational structure adopted by such firms, with the distinguishing features being the degree of centralised control and also the extent to which the worldwide partnership is dominated by the UK/US axis. Wu and Hackett (1977) have analysed the different strategies used in the internationalisation process, ranked in order of popularity from agency/correspondence relation-ships through licensing agreements and making local firms members of the international partnership, to starting an

accounting office from scratch, and finally to various forms
of joint venture (minority interest, equal shares, majority
interest). The structures and strategies of the international
auditing firms are discussed in more detail in Chapter 15.
Consequently, one type of international auditing firm
involves a worldwide partnership with strong centralised
control and whose preferred mode of entry into new
countries is either starting from scratch or effectively 'taking
over' an existing local firm. At the opposite end of the scale
is the international firm which is a fairly loose grouping of
correspondent firms, usually practising under their local
name as well as under the name of the umbrella organisation
(which has little real authority or power). These extreme
polarised cases are less common than the variety of forms
found at different points along the scale.

The relevance of the above discussion to the subject
matter of this chapter is as follows. Where a relatively high
degree of centralised control exists (applying to auditing
standards and procedures as well as to commercial and
administrative objectives), then using the work of an
overseas partner of the same firm is basically the same as
using the work of a partner in a different location in the UK.
Consequently, the problems of 'using the work of another
auditor' do not arise. However, where the international
auditing firm is a collection of correspondent firms each with
a strong national identity and subject to little or no
centralised control, then (although such arrangements may
have compensating benefits) there *is* a problem in using the
work of an overseas partner, as (by definition) common
standards and procedures cannot be assumed to exist. The
danger of generalisation in the case of international auditing
firms should therefore be apparent, as significant differences
in organisational structures exist.

To summarise this section, it seems that the cut-off point
for determining the existence of 'another auditor' is at the
point where there is no centralised control over auditing

standards and procedures. This definition and the above discussion is hinted at in the 'Definition of terms' appendix to the ICAS Statement (1976), where the key phrase is 'operationally distinct'.

12.3 ACCESS TO THE OTHER AUDITOR'S WORK

Before the primary auditor can evaluate the work of the secondary auditor, he must have *access* to that work. In the UK, until the Companies Act 1976 no one was specifically responsible for facilitating such access, and any information and explanations given by the overseas auditor was largely a matter of courtesy rather than compulsion.

This created a serious problem, because in many cases there was no recourse to professional sanctions (that is, in cases where the overseas auditor was not a member of one of the section 161 bodies). Such difficulties of access, combined with the different perceptions of auditing outlined in Section 11.3, meant that in certain instances the MNC auditor could only guess at the auditing standards and procedures being used in overseas locations.

This problem was solved by section 18 of the Companies Act 1976. This makes the directors of the parent company responsible for ensuring that the primary auditor has access to the work of the overseas auditor. The actual wording of the legislation states that (in the case of a subsidiary which is not incorporated in Great Britain) 'it shall be the duty of the holding company, if required by its auditors to do so, to take all such steps as are reasonably open to it to obtain from the subsidiary such information and explanation as aforesaid'. 'Such information and explanation as aforesaid' means such information and explanation as the holding company auditors may reasonably require for the purposes of their duties as auditors of the holding company. If the holding company fails to comply with this section then it 'and every officer thereof who is in default' is guilty of an offence. Although the maximum fine for such an offence is only £200 (and may thus seem of little consequence), the important point is that the responsibility for facilitating access to the secondary auditor's work is now clearly defined, and the primary auditor now has legal backing to his request for information and explanations concerning the audit of the overseas subsidiary. The access problem is therefore considered to have been solved for UK MNCs by the provisions of the Companies Act 1976.

12.4 ASSURANCE AS TO QUALITY OF WORK

As the primary auditor is responsible for the audit opinion given on the MNC's financial statements, he must be certain that the secondary auditor's work is of a suitable quality to support his own overall conclusion. Procedures for reaching this assurance as to the quality of the secondary auditor's work are laid down in the professional literature (AISG, 1969; AICPA, 1972; ICAS, 1976; IFAC, 1981; *UEC, 1978*). The main elements of these procedures can be summarised as follows:

(1) Determine the secondary auditor's reputation for professional competence and integrity. Evidence of this will be a mixture of objective information (for example, membership of a recognised body of accountants) and subjective opinions (for example, informal discussions with mutual contacts);

(2) ensure that the secondary auditor meets the UK independence requirements;

(3) determine the scope of work of the secondary auditor, to ensure that no restrictions were placed on the nature or extent of his audit work; and

(4) consider the secondary auditor's detailed auditing procedures and their results, to ensure that sufficient audit
evidence exists to support the conclusions reached.

The professional literature suggests that point 4 above can
be satisfied by oral and/or written communication. This may
be supported if desired by a review by the primary auditor of
some or all of the secondary auditor's working papers. In
some international auditing firms written communication
with the secondary auditor includes a request to complete a
standard questionnaire. This questionnaire normally covers
certain general matters and also includes specific questions
on the nature and extent and results of the work done in
each audit area. Although these questionnaires can be of
considerable use in providing a summary of the secondary
auditor's work, they are subject to the limitations and
disadvantages of any standardised questionnaire and they
are now used less frequently than in the past. The drawbacks
are recognised in the professional literature. For example,
the ICAS Statement (1976) warns that such questionnaires
should be used with care. The ICAS Statement justifies this
warning by going on to say that such questionnaires may not
be particularly helpful unless they are:

(a) suitably compiled with the specific circumstances of
the group in mind (including the degree of control
exercised over the subsidiary and associated companies);
(b) discussed in advance with the secondary auditors; and
(c) properly completed. (ICAS, 1976, paragraph 19)

The questions in such questionnaires may be duplicated in a
similar questionnaire completed by the primary auditor
when reviewing the secondary auditor's working papers.

This brief review of the professional literature discloses a
common approach to the problem and its solutions. However, this apparent harmony is subject to criticism on two

points, namely (i) the costs of 'double-checking', and (ii) possible conflict between different audit approaches and procedures. These are dealt with in the next two sections.

Finally, the review of the professional literature reveals that the APC has not issued an Auditing Guideline on the topic. The APC has been criticised for this by Hamilton (1978), who considers the absence of a specific Auditing Guideline to be a 'sizeable and unfortunate omission'. However, Gemmell (1978) has replied to this by saying that the APC's priority was to issue pronouncements on the major areas (that is, those dealt with in the original Auditing Standards and Guidelines). Gemmell argues that publication of these 'basic' pronouncements would have been unduly delayed if the APC had widened its scope to include other issues at this initial stage. The current position is that the APC is in the process of developing an Auditing Guideline on the topic, under the heading of 'reliance on other auditors'. Coincidentally, the chairman of the relevant APC working party is Jim Gemmell, author of the article referred to earlier in this paragraph. The Auditing Guideline is still in its initial stages, and publication of the final document is not expected until mid-1985.

12.5 COSTS OF REVIEWING THE WORK OF ANOTHER AUDITOR

Concern has been expressed at the apparent duplication of effort involved in 'auditing the auditors'. This concern has been voiced by the Hundred Group (1981) and also by some of the finance directors interviewed by Lothian in his research study (1983). The Hundred Group consists of a number of chartered accountants employed in senior positions in British industry. Their working party's report stated that it was common for the overseas subsidiaries of MNCs to be audited by firms other than the parent company auditor.

The working party decided that no general rule could be laid down as to whether a single firm should carry out all audits worldwide or whether different firms should be used in particular countries. However, the report notes that members of the Hundred Group have expressed concern at the apparent duplication where one auditor spends time satisfying himself on the work of another auditor of good professional standing and competence. This concern was echoed to some extent in the comments recorded by Lothian (1983), who interviewed the finance directors of nineteen Scottish companies, some of whom were subsidiaries of overseas parent companies. One of the comments was on the 'big firms' review techniques where the client "has to stand aside and watch the firm's review team auditing the auditors, all at his expense" '. Although this comment was aimed specifically at review procedures within a single audit firm, the comment perhaps indicates a more widespread disillusionment with the costs of professional quality control procedures.

Such criticisms say in effect that the opinion reached by the secondary auditor is based on his professional judgement and should be accepted as such by the other professional involved (that is, by the primary auditor). However, this criticism ignores the fact that in an international context 'professional judgement' is largely a product of the local accounting and auditing environment, and this may differ significantly from the UK environment. A review of the secondary auditor's work is therefore necessary to establish that UK requirements have been met. To avoid misunderstandings and to pre-empt criticism, the primary auditor should make it clear to the MNC parent company that a 'review' is precisely that, that is, it is an attempt to evaluate the extent to which reliance can be placed on the secondary auditor's work, and it is not merely a repetition of the secondary auditor's examination.

Another criticism of such reviews is the duplication (and

therefore costs) involved where audit firm *A* reviews the work of firm *B* for the audit of the overseas subsidiaries of two separate MNCs. This criticism is based on the proposition that if *A's* review of the audit of the overseas subsidiary of one MNC shows that the audit was performed satisfactorily, then this can be taken as evidence that *B's* overall quality control procedures are operating satisfactorily; consequently, *A* can assume that *B's* quality control procedures have also ensured that the audit of the overseas subsidiary of the other MNC has been performed satisfactorily. ('Quality control' is usually defined as the set of policies and procedures which the auditing firm has adopted to ensure compliance with professional standards – see for example Goerdeler, 1981.) However, if *A* has not specifically reviewed *B's* quality control procedures, then *A* might be reluctant to conclude that *B's* satisfactory performance was evidence of a system of quality control. One possible solution is for *A's* review of the audit of one overseas subsidiary to include a specific review of *B's* quality control procedures. If this direct test of *B's* quality control procedures is satisfactory, then it seems reasonable to suggest that *A* can assume that *B's* quality control procedures will be applied to the other overseas subsidiary in question. This would result in a consequent reduction in *A's* review of the audit of that other overseas subsidiary. This solution seems particularly relevant in the case of the major auditing firms, which frequently need to use each other's work and reports.

A peer review programme (whereby regular inter-firm reviews of quality control are performed) would allow a significant reduction in the amount of detailed work needed in the review of another auditor's work. A peer review programme is also intended to be seen as part of the profession's self-regulating process, hence reducing the need for external (that is, governmental) regulation (Olson, 1980). However, at present a formal system of peer review exists only in the US, the requirement having been introduced by AICPA in 1977. Stamp (1979) considers that the European accountancy profession remains unconvinced as to the value and effectiveness of peer reviews.

12.6 DIFFERENCES IN AUDIT PROCEDURES

This section discusses the problems raised when the secondary auditor uses significantly different audit procedures. Audit procedures are defined as the methods of collecting and evaluating the evidence used to support the audit opinion.

One example of differences in audit procedures occurs where the primary auditor uses a systems-based audit approach, relying heavily on an evaluation of the accounting systems and internal control, with only a minimum of substantive audit tests, and where the secondary auditor performs only a brief systems review and relies mainly on substantive tests. (A number of auditing textbooks, such as Arens and Loebbecke (1976), provide details of specific auditing procedures.) Another example concerns the sampling methods used. The primary auditor may use statistical sampling techniques (such as monetary unit sampling, as described for example in Black and Eastwood, 1980) which permit him to reach a statistically-valid conclusion as to the maximum monetary error in the financial statements, in relation to a certain level of confidence. However, the secondary auditor may use judgement samples. A third example is where the primary auditor is in the habit of circularising creditors to obtain direct confirmation of amounts owed, and where the secondary auditor uses alternative methods. These specific examples show the general problem faced by the primary auditor when the secondary auditor uses different audit procedures. The general problem is that the primary auditor must evaluate the results of audit procedures with which he may be unfamiliar and which he may have rejected in the past as being inadequate.

The preliminary stage of the solution would seem to lie in the primary auditor obtaining a proper understanding of the different procedures used. The basis of the solution should then be an analysis of why his firm does not use the secondary auditor's procedure. If on the one hand the reason was personal preference for one of two equally acceptable procedures, then the primary auditor is effectively saying that the secondary auditor's procedure is a satisfactory alternative, and hence no further work is required. If on the other hand the secondary auditor's procedure is not used by the primary auditor because he considers that it does not meet the criterion of producing sufficient audit evidence, then he must ask the secondary auditor to perform additional audit work. In extreme cases the primary auditor will need to carry out this additional work himself. Maximum efficiency will be obtained if a review of the secondary auditor's procedures is performed in the planning stage of the audit. This will ensure the proper timing of any additional work required.

12.7   SUMMARY

This chapter has discussed the auditing standards transfer problem from the perspective of the differences in auditing firms (rather than the differences in *countries* as in Chapter 11). This discussion has shown that in some cases there may be problems in using the work of another auditor even when that auditor is a member of the same international auditing firm (see Section 12.2).

The professional literature recognises the existence of the problems involved in using the work of another auditor, and the major international and regional bodies have issued statements on the subject. The UK approach is contained in statements issued by the section 161 bodies in 1976, although the APC plans to replace these statements by 1985. The general approach adopted in the professional literature is summarised in Section 12.4.

As noted briefly in Section 12.5, the problem of using the work of another auditor can be seen in the wider context of the profession's attitude to quality control. One solution could therefore be an international system of peer review, based perhaps on an extension of the AICPA programme, to ensure compliance with a set of internationally agreed auditing standards. This could be further refined by the Big Nine firms being judged against a more rigorous set of auditing standards (for example, in such a way as to mean that compliance with this more rigorous international set of auditing standards would automatically mean compliance with any particular country's set of auditing standards). Although it may seem impossible to impose such a solution on the present international environment (where attempts at harmonisation of auditing standards are a relatively recent development), it is possible to envisage a more organic way of reaching this outcome, with the first step being, for example, the Big Nine firms adapting the present AICPA peer review programme to encompass a combined US/UK set of auditing standards. Such an international system of peer review would help to achieve the international auditing profession's perceived desire for improved quality control. It would also minimise the amount of time spent by the international auditing firms in detailed reviews of each other's work, thereby answering the criticisms raised of the cost of such work.

The differences in audit procedures mentioned in Section 12.6 can best be resolved through the moves towards international harmonisation, which attempts to establish a minimum set of acceptable audit procedures. International harmonisation is discussed further in Chapter 13.

13 International Harmonisation

13.1 INTRODUCTION

The harmonisation issue is relevant to the two main themes of this book, namely the audit of MNCs and comparative international auditing. First, supporters of the international harmonisation of auditing standards claim that harmonisation would solve many of the problems discussed in Chapters 11 and 12. (These chapters dealt with the conceptual and practical problems involved in ensuring that an MNC's overseas subsidiaries are audited in accordance with the parent company's national auditing standards.) Secondly, the need for harmonisation arises from differences in national auditing standards. (Chapters 3 to 10 analyse auditing standards in certain selected countries.) This explains briefly why the harmonisation issue is worthy of consideration. Harmonisation is usually taken to mean a gradual convergence through the narrowing of differences. Harmonisation does not necessarily mean strict uniformity.

The rest of this chapter is structured as follows. Section 13.2 analyses the rationale underlying the need for harmonisation. Section 13.3 discusses theoretical and practical barriers to progress. Section 13.4 deals with the major harmonising influences that exist. This section concentrates mainly on IFAC, but also looks briefly at the impact of the EEC, the *UEC,* and the Big Nine international auditing firms. Finally, Section 13.5 provides a summary and conclusions.

13.2   THE NEED FOR HARMONISATION

Chapter 2 explained first why there is a need for auditing, and secondly why there is a need for auditing standards. This section explains why there is a need for international harmonisation of auditing standards.

The need for international harmonisation of auditing standards arises from the same source as the need for auditing standards set out in Section 2.3. That section put forward the argument that an international user of financial statements needs to know the auditing standards governing the conduct of an MNC's audit, in order to judge the quality of the audit and hence to determine the extent to which the audit does in fact 'add credibility' to the financial statements. This argument concluded that *codified* auditing standards were required to fulfil this information need. In the case of an international user attempting to analyse and compare financial statements from several countries, some of which have codified auditing standards which are markedly diverse and some of which have no codified auditing standards at all, it seems difficult if not impossible to construct a decision model which incorporates these differences into a comparative assessment of the reliability of the information contained in the financial statements. However, if only one set of auditing standards were used around the world, then the international user would be able to place the same reliance on audits performed in different countries, and consequently could use with equal confidence the information contained in financial statements from different countries.

The argument for harmonisation of auditing standards is therefore that it is a necessary condition for facilitating the international comparison of financial statements. This of course begs the question as to why it is considered necessary or desirable to facilitate the international comparison of financial statements.

The specific answer from the investor's viewpoint is that such international comparison will assist him in achieving significant risk reduction through the international divers- ification of his share portfolio. Solnik (1974) and Lessard (1976) describe the risk reduction that can be achieved through international diversification. The more general answer from the economic viewpoint is that if the business community can rely on the financial statements of com- panies in other countries then the business community will be more likely to increase international trade and invest- ment by buying or selling goods and services, lending or investing. Poor comparability of financial statements can be seen as a barrier to the free international movement of goods and capital. In an ideal world such barriers would be removed in order to achieve an optimal allocation of production factors and thus maximise economic welfare. Even though it is recognised that in certain cases barriers to movement of goods and capital may be justified on the grounds of achieving particular national economic or politi- cal goals, a 'second-best' international solution may be reached by removing unjustified and unnecessary distortions such as those caused by the non-comparability of financial statements. This economic analysis of the need for inter- national comparability of financial statements provides the fundamental rationale underlying the need for the inter- national harmonisation of auditing standards.

Although the preceding paragraphs analyse the compara- bility issue from a global perspective, the analysis can also be applied on a regional basis. The most obvious example of this is the European Economic Community, which has incorporated harmonisation of auditing standards and the improved comparability of financial statements into its overall objectives of achieving economic integration. This relationship operates as follows:

(1)   The company law harmonisation programme (in par-

ticular the Fourth, Seventh and Eighth Directives, dealing with form and contents of accounts, group accounts and auditors) is intended first, to encourage the free movement of factors of production, especially captial; and secondly, to secure the right of establishment, whereby there are no barriers to entry that prevent an individual or company setting up in business in another member state.

(2)   The free movement of factors and the right of establishment combine with the EEC's other activities (for example, agricultural policy, transport policy, industrial policy, monetary policy, elimination of customs duties and quotas) in order to produce literally a 'common market'. In theory, this free trade area would have no tariffs between member countries, would have a common external tariff and would have free movement of *factors* as well as *products*.

(3)   This 'common market' combines with the attempts to integrate economic policy in order to achieve the EEC's specific objectives (set out in Article 2 of the Treaty of Rome), which are to promote:

- a harmonious development of economic activities;
- a continuous and balanced expansion;
- increased stability;
- an accelerated raising of the standard of living.

The comparability aspect of the company law harmonisation programme is therefore not an end in itself, but only a means to the end of economic integration. This shows on a regional basis how the comparability of financial statements is an essential component of the overall economic strategy.

In addition to the comparability aspect outlined above, international harmonisation would to a large extent solve the problems discussed in Chapter 11 (Transferring auditing standards overseas) and Chapter 12 (Using the work of another auditor). This is because the domestic auditing standards and the overseas auditing standards would now be similar in form and content, and consequently the MNC's auditor could be confident that the audits of the overseas subsidiaries were being performed in accordance with much the same auditing standards as used for the parent company.

These arguments in favour of international harmonisation are subjected to a critical assessment in the following section.

13.3 CRITICISMS OF HARMONISATION

In most cases, the literature on harmonisation of auditing standards either takes the desirability of harmonisation for granted or devotes a few paragraphs to showing why the evidence in favour of harmonisation is incontrovertible. In general, the literature on harmonisation is remarkably uncritical, and spends little time on questioning whether harmonisation is in fact the panacea it is assumed to be. This section attempts to rectify this by providing a critical assessment of the arguments for harmonisation as set out in the previous section.

13.3.1 Reasons for International Differences

The first point to make is that the present international differences in auditing standards are not purely arbitrary, but occur because national auditing standards have arisen in response to local influences from the legal, business and social environments. As these environments differ around the world, it is perhaps not surprising that auditing standards develop in different ways and at different rates. If these differences in local influences are fundamental, then the harmonisation of auditing standards will treat the symptoms rather than the cause and will merely produce a superficial semblance of similarity. If the externally-imposed 'harmonised' auditing standards do not correspond to those produced by the local environmental factors, then these underlying influences would be expected to resurface eventually. This would probably lead to the 'harmonised' auditing standards being rejected or ignored.

13.3.2 No Overall Context for International Harmonisation

The second criticism is that international harmonisation does not fit into a defined framework of economic and political objectives. Although it is relatively easy in the case of the EEC to trace the relationship between the harmonisation of auditing and accounting standards and the overall objective of economic integration, it is not possible to identify such a relationship in the international case. Although the analysis in the previous section explained the need for the international comparability of financial statements as a means to removing the barriers to the free movement of capital, there is no worldwide organisation (comparable to the EEC at the regional level) that has the power or the authority to develop a worldwide 'common market' with harmonised laws and integrated economic policies. Without the support of other harmonising elements in an overall structure, it could be argued that the impact of harmonisation will be minimal.

13.3.3 International Differences in Accounting Principles

A third criticism of international harmonisation of auditing standards is that such harmonisation cannot be expected to contribute much to the international comparability of financial statements when these financial statements are prepared using fundamentally different accounting measurement and disclosure practices. If auditing standards are harmonised, then even though the international user of financial statements may be able to place equal reliance on the *credibility* of the information in two sets of financial statements, this may be of little use if the information has been prepared on the basis of fundamentally different accounting policies. The contribution of the IASC to achieving international comparability via the harmonisation of *accounting* principles is therefore crucial. However, it should be noted that harmonisation of accounting standards is subject to the same criticisms outlined in 13.3.1 and 13.3.2 above.

13.3.4 Loss of National Sovereignty

It may be claimed that the existence of an international set of auditing standards is of benefit to countries where the auditing profession is not sufficiently advanced or has insufficient resources to develop its own set of standards. However, it could be argued conversely that some countries will resent and resist the external imposition of such standards, considering it to involve a loss of sovereignty and control over what occurs within their boundaries. This could arise from mere jingoism or from a deeper understanding of the different environmental influences outlined in 13.3.1 above. The danger of such a conflict might be averted to some extent by ensuring that all countries participate in the decision-making process and also agree to abide by whatever voting procedures are laid down in the constitution of the harmonising body to which they belong.

13.3.5 Separate Auditing Standards for MNCs

Although it was argued that international harmonisation

would help to solve the problems discussed in Chapters 11 and 12, it might be considered that since the problems arise in the audits of MNCs, then the solution should be not international harmonisation, but rather a separate set of internationally-agreed auditing standards for MNC audits. This would mean that auditing standards for uninational companies would more fully reflect national environmental influences, whereas auditing standards for MNCs would reflect the influences of the international business environment. However, this does not solve the problem of uninational companies that attract foreign investors. These investors would benefit more from fully harmonised international auditing standards than from a set of internationally-agreed MNC auditing standards.

13.3.6 Conclusion

The above criticisms of international harmonisation of auditing standards indicate that harmonisation may not be the universal cure which it is frequently assumed to be. The major criticism seems to be that outlined in 13.3.1 (Reasons for International Differences). The ultimate importance of this criticism depends on how fundamental are the differences in national influences on auditing standards. It may be that these national influences are being overtaken by international influences, such as the effect of increasing international portfolio and direct investment, and the increasing influence of international accounting and non-accounting organisations. In this case, we would expect the impact of local differences to be decreasing and less than crucial. However, it is likely that these national environmental differences will continue to be relevant and so cannot be ignored in any theoretical or practical discussion on harmonisation.

13.4 CURRENT INFLUENCES ON HARMONISATION

13.4.1 The EEC

As already mentioned in Section 13.2, the EEC's proposed Eighth Directive deals with auditors. It is concerned mainly with auditors' qualifications (that is, standards of education and training) and standards of independence (Bartholomew, 1978). Although the proposed directive is only concerned with two main issues, it is an extremely powerful harmonising influence since the final directive will have legal force once it is eventually incorporated into the national legislation of member states. However, its slow progress to date indicates the difficulties involved (even within such a relatively small group of countries) in attempting to reach agreement on fundamental issues such as auditor independence, where the different local environments have produced different notions on the extent to which auditors can provide non-auditing services to clients.

13.4.2 The *UEC*

The *UEC (Union Européenne des Experts Comptables Economiques et Financiers)*, whose membership comprises accountancy bodies from eighteen Western European countries, has concerned itself with the harmonisation of auditing standards and practices through the work of its Auditing Statements Board, Professional Ethics Committee, and Education and Professional Training Committee (McDougall (1979)). The *UEC's* pronouncements are addressed to its member bodies, who are then supposed to incorporate them into their own national pronouncements. However, there is no formal mechanism for ensuring that the *UEC's* pronouncements *are* incorporated in this way,

nor are there any sanctions for non-incorporation. Consequently, the *UEC's* authority is rather limited. It is difficult
to envisage an optimistic future for the *UEC,* as it lacks any
legal backing for its pronouncements (cf. the EEC) and also
lacks the status of a truly international body (cf. IFAC).

13.4.3   The Big Nine

The Big Nine international auditing firms could also be
considered to be a harmonising influence. As well as an
indirect contribution through membership and support of
the international professional bodies, their domination of
the MNC audit market (see for example Lafferty and
Cairns, 1980) gives them an incentive to provide a *direct*
contribution to harmonisation. This incentive occurs because if their international offices are involved in the audits
of MNCs (and their subsidiaries) then there is a need to
ensure that the audit standards and procedures used in each
office are above a certain minimum level. The simplest way
of ensuring this is to adopt a uniform set of standards and
procedures. However, although this incentive may have
provided some positive harmonising influence, two caveats
must be borne in mind. First, although the audit of MNCs'
subsidiaries may be performed to a standardised pattern,
there is not necessarily the same incentive to audit local
companies in accordance with this pattern. This is especially
the case where local audit requirements are less strict than
those embodied in the international firm's standardised
approach, as the firm may consider that the cost of applying
the stricter standardised approach outweighs the benefits. It
may be therefore that the Big Nine only influence the
harmonisation of MNCs' auditing standards. This could be
seen as a further argument in favour of separate auditing
standards for MNCs, as discussed above in 13.3.5. Secondly,
as noted in Chapter 15, some of the Big Nine firms are loose

collections of very independent national firms. Consequently, the international auditing firm's ability to impose a uniform set of auditing standards and practices may be limited.

13.4.4 IFAC

The International Federation of Accountants (IFAC) was established in 1977 at the international congress of accountants in Munich. It succeeded (and significantly enlarged the scope of) the International Co-ordination Committee for the Accounting Profession (ICCAP), which was established as a result of the consensus reached at the previous international congress in Sydney in 1972. (ICCAP itself came into existence as a result of the recommendations of an international working party set up at the previous international congress in Paris in 1967.) This brief history highlights the influence of the international congresses as a forum for discussion and for action. However, the intention of IFAC is to enable agreement to be reached on international issues in a more formal manner and on a quicker time-scale than is possible at the five-yearly congresses. Chetkovich (1979) and Goerdeler (1979) provide a more detailed introduction to the history of IFAC.

IFAC's broad objective is stated in its constitution as 'the development and enhancement of a co-ordinated worldwide accountancy profession with harmonised standards' (IFAC, 1977). This overall objective is then defined further in the constitution to include three main aims:

(1) to establish international technical, ethical and educational guidelines for the accountancy profession;
(2) to develop regional organisations with common objectives; and
(3) to arrange international congresses of accountants,

which are intended to facilitate discussion and reach conclusions on desired common aims.

These general objectives are broken down into more specific terms in IFAC's twelve-point work programme (listed in Sempier, 1979). This work programme is to be carried out through its seven committees, which deal with auditing, education, ethics, international congresses, management accounting, planning and regional organisations. In addition to outlining its objectives, IFAC's constitution also prescribes its structure, which consists of two governing bodies. First, there is the Assembly, which consists of one representative from each member body, of which there were originally fifty, from forty countries. Secondly, there is the Council, consisting of fifteen representatives from fifteen countries. These representatives are elected at ordinary meetings of the Assembly. Although the Assembly is the senior governing body, it delegates extensive powers to the Council. The latter body elects from its members a president, a deputy-president and two vice-presidents.

The constitution also sets out IFAC's sources of finance, which come from a scaled set of annual contributions from the member bodies. The budget covers the salary costs of IFAC's secretariat, which consists of only three full-time employees, and other administrative costs. However, this is a misleading representation of the true costs of IFAC's activities, as travelling expenses are borne separately by member bodies. Also, the premises and certain overheads of its administrative office in New York are supplied by the AICPA. An indication of the significance of travelling expenses is given by Volten (1979), who says that the Dutch Institute's travelling expenses on Council business and Auditing Practices Committee business are eleven times the Dutch annual scale contribution. Such expense may discourage the accountancy bodies with minimal resources from seeking membership of the Council and the Committees.

As far as IFAC's progress towards harmonisation of international auditing standards is concerned, the main achievement has been the publication of international auditing guidelines by IFAC's International Auditing Practices Committee (IAPC). By the end of 1983 the IAPC had issued the following guidelines:

(1) Objective and scope of the audit of financial statements
(2) Audit engagement letters
(3) Basic principles governing an audit
(4) Planning
(5) Using the work of another auditor
(6) Study and evaluation of the accounting system and related internal controls in connection with an audit
(7) Control of the quality of audit work
(8) Audit evidence
(9) Documentation
(10) Using the work of an internal auditor
(11) Fraud and error
(12) Analytical review
(13) The auditor's report on financial statements

The authority of the guidelines is in the nature of recommendations rather than requirements. The preface to the series of guidelines (IFAC, 1979) states that the IAPC will 'seek to promote their voluntary acceptance'. If any differences exist between national regulations and the guidelines, then the member bodies should implement the guidelines 'when and to the extent practicable'. The UK profession has responded to this by agreeing to incorporate the principles on which IFAC's auditing guidelines are based into the UK Auditing Standards and Guidelines (paragraph 16 of the explanatory foreword to the Auditing Standards and Guidelines, ICAS, 1980).

The above description of IFAC's objectives, structure and progress provides a background against which to analyse critically the aims and achievements of IFAC. The first point to note is that IFAC's objective of creating a worldwide accountancy profession is more comprehensive and more ambitious than merely harmonising international auditing standards. IFAC is concerned with the *accountancy* profession rather than the auditing profession. This distinction is important when one considers the difficulties encountered at national level, for example in the UK, in reaching agreement on what constitutes 'the profession'. These difficulties are likely to be magnified at the international level, and it may seem that the task of creating a worldwide *auditing* profession is sufficiently difficult to preclude any time or energy being spent on harmonising the international *accountancy* profession. Conversely, it could be argued that international harmonisation of auditing standards and accountancy standards are mutually dependent, and hence the best long-term strategy is to create a harmonised accountancy profession with common aims and attitudes concerning both auditing *and* accounting. In addition, it may be argued that there is a need for an international professional body in order to provide a higher profile and a more powerful voice in the international arena, especially considering the growing influence of international non-accounting organisations (in particular the United Nations).

The second point concerns how quickly and how rigorously the IAPC guidelines are incorporated into the pronouncements of member bodies. It has already been noted that IFAC's role is persuasive rather than prescriptive, and the phrase 'when and to the extent practicable' in the preface to the guidelines seems to leave scope for a wide range of interpretations as to how soon, and how much of, the guidelines should be adopted locally. The member bodies may consider harmonisation to be a good idea in theory but not when they are faced with its practical consequences. If the international auditing guidelines become international only in name and not in nature, then the international business community may dismiss the entire harmonisation exercise and ignore any positive results IFAC may have achieved. If IFAC is to establish and maintain its credibility, it should perhaps indicate periodically the extent to which the guidelines are being adopted by the member bodies.

The third point concerns the extent to which international auditing standards will be harmonised by the present guidelines, assuming that they are adopted in full by the member bodies. Because they are guidelines rather than attempts at rigid standardisation, they are open to differing interpretations in different countries. The problem from the harmonisation aspect is that these local interpretations will be influenced by national rather than international viewpoints. It could happen that all member bodies believe they are complying with the guidelines but they are actually interpreting them in materially different ways. Consequently, the international user of accounts may be faced with decidedly unharmonised auditing standards.

Perhaps the major problem facing IFAC is that there is no such person as the 'international user of accounts' – there is only a number of *national* users from different countries. As a result, there is no unique 'international' user perception of concepts such as auditor independence.

Reinhard Goerdeler, IFAC's first president, has gone on record as saying that absolute worldwide uniformity will never be possible (Goerdeler, 1979). He attributes this to the fact that accounting and auditing must continue to reflect regional and national differences in business practices, legal systems and economic environments. However, he considers that international standards can achieve first, a narrowing of differences that are not fully reflective of international environments and secondly, an understanding and communication of the nature of and reasons for remaining differences.

13.5 SUMMARY

Chapter 13 started by analysing the reasons for the international harmonisation of auditing standards. International harmonisation was seen as a necessary step towards improving the international allocation of resources via increased comparability of financial statements. The main objection to harmonisation was considered to be the fundamental differences in the national environments which created the different auditing standards. Superficial attempts at harmonisation would therefore treat the symptoms rather than the cause, and would be of little long-term benefit. The major influences on harmonisation were then discussed, concentrating on IFAC, but also with reference to the EEC, the *UEC* and the Big Nine international auditing firms.

The arguments outlined in this chapter seem to lead to two main conclusions. First, the full benefits of harmonised auditing standards can only be attained if attempts are made to harmonise the underlying legal and economic environments. Such a programme requires the authority and power of a body with sufficient legal force, and so may be feasible for the EEC but not for IFAC.

Secondly, if it is accepted that IFAC cannot harmonise auditing differences arising from such fundamentally different environmental influences, then IFAC's main contribution to the international harmonisation of auditing standards should be as follows:

(1) the removal of auditing differences *not* caused by fundamentally different legal and economic environments; and

(2) the analysis and communication of what these fundamental auditing differences are and how they affect the reliance to be placed on audited international financial statements.

Although a body such as IFAC may not wish to draw attention to the importance of the areas which it is incapable of harmonising, this analysis and communication would be a significant contribution to increased international understanding of differences and similarities in auditing standards and hence to improved comparability of international financial statements.

14 The Audit of MNCs' Non-Financial Information

14.1 INTRODUCTION

This chapter deals with an emerging issue in international auditing, namely the publication and audit of non-financial information (NFI) in the annual reports of MNCs. Although this issue has developed only recently, it is likely to become increasingly important in the future, particularly to MNCs operating in less-developed countries, and to their auditors.

The term 'non-financial information' is usually taken to mean any information in the annual report apart from the financial statements. Financial statements are usually defined as the balance sheet, income statement, funds statement and accompanying notes. The meaning of NFI in a particular country depends partly on what that country requires to be disclosed in the financial statements. However, NFI can in general be taken to include such matters as the following:

- Employment matters (such as employment policies, statistics for various categories, training schemes)
- Production (such as units produced, materials and components consumed)
- Organisation structure (such as details of subsidiaries and associates, directors and management)
- Environmental measures (such as pollution control)

Such information may be past or future orientated. NFI overlaps to a large extent with social reporting, where the latter term is defined in its widest sense to include all matters concerning the company's relationships with society at large.

The theme of this book is international auditing, taken to include the audit of MNCs and auditing in other countries. Consequently, this chapter concentrates on the international aspects of the publication and audit of NFI. International aspects include comparative data on the publication and audit of NFI. International aspects also include the NFI published by MNCs, not only in the annual reports of the MNC parent companies but also the annual reports of overseas subsidiaries.

The remaining sections of this chapter deal with the main issues as follows. Section 14.2 discusses the need for NFI. It analyses the origins of the demand for NFI, and places the requirements for NFI in the context of the other control and regulatory mechanisms used by host countries. Section 14.3 describes some national requirements and supranational proposals for the publication of NFI. Section 14.4 analyses the extent to which the traditional auditing function can be expanded to include the audit of NFI.

14.2   THE NEED FOR NFI

The traditional view of corporate reporting in the UK was based on a model of corporate accountability that was restricted to the economic and financial responsibilities entrusted to the directors of a company by its shareholders. The information required to be presented in the corporate report was thus restricted mainly to financial data which enabled the shareholder to assess the extent to which the directors had fulfilled these responsibilities. The shareholder could then reach buy/hold/sell decisions in an assumed attempt to maximise his wealth.

This traditional UK model may not apply to other countries, due to differences in the accounting environment.

For example, in countries such as France or Germany where the law dominates the accounting environment, there seems to be less emphasis than in the UK on the provision of useful information to shareholders and more emphasis on the protection of creditors and lenders. Another example is in countries which require a system of two-tier boards, one tier containing employee representatives. In such countries the model of corporate accountability seems to include a greater degree of responsibility to employees than does the traditional UK model.

Furthermore, the traditional UK model has changed over the last decade or two. Corporate accountability in the UK now seems to be a much wider concept, and includes a greater recognition of the company's *social* responsibility. This change has occurred partly because of the influence of other EEC member states, and partly because of increased pressure from particular interest groups. The concept of corporate *social* responsibility recognises that although a company's actions may be aimed primarily at increasing the wealth of its owners, those actions may also have a significant impact on other parties, such as employees and the general public. As mentioned in Chapter 2, these other parties may be considered as stakeholders, having entrusted certain resources to the company. The normal financial statements may not be sufficient to allow these stakeholders to determine whether the company has fulfilled its perceived social responsibilities, and consequently a demand arises for additional information. This additional information is often of a non-financial nature, reflecting the source of its demand. For example, employees may be interested in details of new products and processes, and local communities may be interested in details of matters, such as pollution, that affect the local environment.

The growing irrelevance of the traditional UK view of corporate reporting is highlighted in the case of a UK MNC's overseas subsidiaries. It is difficult to argue that these subsidiaries are only accountable to their UK parent (and indirectly to the MNC's shareholders). This completely ignores the effects of the subsidiaries' actions on the local economic and social environment. The host country government is unlikely to adopt such a permissive attitude, as it will have implicit or explicit goals that may be in conflict with those of the MNC (R. H. Mason, 1974). Such host country government goals may be concerned with economic growth, inflation, unemployment, balance of payments and rates of technological progress. Some of the MNC's policies may be in direct conflict with these goals. For example, the MNC may prefer to use parent company rather than local personnel. Another example is that if the MNC centralises its research and development function in the parent country, the host country misses the opportunity of participating indirectly in technological advancement. A final example of conflicting goals is where the MNC uses a system of transfer pricing as a means of minimising tax payments to host governments.

Such real or perceived conflict has led to increased regulation and control of MNCs by host governments (Hood and Young, 1979, chapters 5 and 6). Host governments frequently carry out these regulatory actions in isolation (that is, without co-ordinating their actions with those of other governments). This may lead to the MNC deciding to move out to a less hostile environment, thus depriving the original host country of a source of income and employment. Consequently, host countries (particularly less-developed countries) perceive benefits in establishing a worldwide set of minimum behavioural standards for MNCs. This explains the efforts being made in this field by the United Nations.

Host country regulation of MNCs falls into two distinct categories. First, there is direct regulation, where the host government uses its legislative powers to alter the MNC's actions. An extreme form of direct regulation would be nationalisation of the MNC's overseas subsidiary. Another example of direct regulation is a tax system that discriminates against foreign-owned enterprises. Direct regulation could also include legal requirements for host country citizens to form a certain percentage of the MNC's workforce or management.

The second category of host country regulation is *indirect* regulation. In this case the host country government requires the MNC subsidiary to disclose in its annual report its policies and activities in key areas, such as employment, production, and research and development. Indirect regulation is basically persuasive rather than prescriptive, in that the MNC is not being directed to carry out specific actions. A system of indirect regulation operates on the assumption that an MNC will seek to avoid any adverse publicity that may arise from the disclosure of activities and policies that are socially unacceptable (according to host country norms). If an MNC wishes to avoid adverse reactions, then its alternatives would normally be either to avoid disclosure or to amend its behaviour. However, the system of indirect regulation prohibits the first alternative, and so (according to the theory) the MNC is constrained to amend its behaviour to conform to socially acceptable activities. Although indirect regulation is generally persuasive rather than prescriptive, there may be an implicit threat of direct regulation if the MNC's disclosures reveal an unsatisfactory position (measured against some host government ideal).

This chapter deals with the non-financial information disclosures required by indirect regulation.

14.3 INTERNATIONAL REQUIREMENTS AND PROPOSALS

This section concentrates on the proposals issued by supranational organisations such as the EEC, the UN and the Organisation for Economic Co-operation and Develop-

192   *Other Issues in International Auditing*

ment (OECD). Details of particular *national* requirements are provided by Dierkes (1979), Grojer and Stark (1977), Schoenfeld (1978) and Schreuder (1978, 1981). Perhaps the most interesting national development is the 1977 law in France requiring companies to publish a *bilan social*. This report is almost exclusively concerned with employee matters, such as wages, working conditions and industrial relations. Schreuder (1978) refers to the social reports issued voluntarily by certain German companies. A feature of these unregulated reports is that they disclose societal benefits but tend to omit societal costs. Schreuder (1981) says that in the Netherlands a significant number of companies have recently started to publish social reports on a voluntary basis. As in France, these reports focus almost entirely on employee matters.

14.3.1   The United Nations (UN)

The UN has been active in the international accounting arena since the early 1970s. Its principal objective has been to draft a code of conduct for MNCs. (The UN refers to MNCs as transnational corporations or TNCs.) Part of this code of conduct deals with disclosure of information by MNCs, and part of this disclosure relates to the disclosure of NFI. Most of the work on information disclosure has been carried out under the aegis of the UN Commission on Transnational Corporations. The Commission's objectives include securing effective international arrangements for the operations of MNCs and furthering the understanding of the nature and effects of the activities of MNCs.

Disclosure of NFI is a key element of two reports published by the UN. The first report was presented to the UN in 1977 by the Group of Experts on International Standards of Accounting and Reporting (United Nations, 1977). This report (sometimes referred to as the 'Blue

Book') consisted of a suggested set of international standards of accounting and reporting. These standards included a list of minimum items to be disclosed in the general purpose report (that is, the annual report), with Part I of the list referring to financial information and Part II referring to non-financial information. The NFI disclosures are grouped under the following headings:

(1) Labour and employment
(2) Production
(3) Investment programme
(4) Organisational structure
(5) Environmental measures

Each heading includes two lists of specific disclosure items, one (Section A) for the enterprise as a whole and one (Section B) for individual member companies within the group. The list of items in Section B is more comprehensive than in Section A, presumably because certain information is more relevant at a disaggregated level. Because the Group of Experts' report represents the most comprehensive set of NFI disclosures suggested by a supranational body, the complete list of items for individual companies (Section B) is given below.

(1) *Labour and employment*
(a) Description of labour relations policy
    (i)   Trade union recognition*
    (ii) Complaints and dispute settlement mechanism and procedure*
(b) Number of employees as at year end and annual average
(c) Number employed by function (professional, production etc.)
(d) Number of women employees by function
(e) Number of national employees by function
(f) Average hours worked per week

(g) Labour turnover, annual rate

(h) Absenteeism – working hours lost (number and as percentage of total working hours per year)

(i) Accident rate (describe basis)

(j) Description of health and safety standards

(k) Employee costs
   (i) Total wages, salaries and other payments to employees (before tax)
   (ii) Social expenditures paid to institutions and Government for benefit of workers (excluding pension schemes reported in the profit and loss statement)
   (iii) Summary description and cost of training programmes

* For reporting of these items, reference may be made to the application of national laws, agreements with trade unions or publicly available written company policies.

(2) *Production*

(a) Description of practices regarding acquisition of raw materials and components (indicate percentage acquired from intercompany foreign sources and percentage from all foreign sources)

(b) Indicate average annual capacity utilisation in accordance with normal industrial practice

(c) Physical output by principal lines of business in accordance with normal industrial practice

(d) Description of significant new products and processes

(3) *Investment programme*

(a) Description of announced new capital expenditure

(b) Description of main projects, including their cost, estimated additions to capacity, estimated direct effect on employment

(c) Description of announced mergers and takeovers, including their cost and estimated direct effect on employment

(4) *Organisational structure*
(a) Names of members of board of directors and, where applicable, the supervisory board and a description of their affiliations with companies outside the group
(b) Number of owners or shareholders and, where known, the names of the principal owners or shareholders

(5) *Environmental measures*
Description of types of major or special environmental measures carried out, together with cost data, where available

The second report was presented to the UN in 1982 by the *Ad Hoc* Intergovernmental Working Group of Experts on International Standards of Accounting and Reporting (*CTC Reporter*, 1983). This group seemed to find it harder to reach a consensus (Zünd, 1983), and its report is basically a diluted version of the 1977 report. One area where consensus *was* reached is that lists of minimum items for disclosure should not follow a predetermined format. Consequently, the 1982 report provides a number of NFI disclosure headings but does not attempt to provide detailed lists under these headings (unlike the 1977 report). The NFI disclosure headings in the 1982 report are as follows:

(1) Labour and employment
(2) Production
(3) Investment programme
(4) Organisational structure
(5) Environmental measures
(6) Value added
(7) Transfer of technology, especially to the developing countries
(8) Observance of legal requirements

The *Ad Hoc* working group also recommended that an international body be established under the auspices of the

UN to continue developments in the international accounting environment. The UN Economic and Social Council adopted this recommendation, and has established an Intergovernmental Working Group of Experts on International Standards of Accounting and Reporting. This group is likely to continue the UN's efforts to improve the quantity and quality of NFI disclosure to MNCs.

The authority of these UN reports is essentially persuasive rather than prescriptive. The ideal from the UN viewpoint would be for each member state to incorporate the standards into its own national legislation. Until this occurs, there are no legal sanctions or other mechanisms for enforcing or monitoring compliance. The preliminary results of a survey (as yet unpublished) carried out by Deloitte Haskins & Sells International in conjunction with the University of Glasgow show that very few countries include a majority (or even a large minority) of the 1977 report's NFI items in their reporting requirements.

14.3.2   The Organisation for Economic Co-operation and Development (OECD)

The OECD proposals on the disclosure of NFI form a small but significant part of its 1976 'Declaration on International Investment and Multinational Enterprises' (OECD, 1976). This declaration includes a number of 'Guidelines for Multinational Enterprises', including one on disclosure of information. The other guidelines deal with general policies, competition, financing, taxation, employment and industrial relations, and science and technology.

The guideline on disclosure of information recommends that enterprises should publish on a regular basis the following information relating to the enterprise as a whole:

(1) Organisation structure, including details of parent company and affiliates

(2) Geographical areas of operations, and principal activities therein
(3) Operating results and sales by geographical area, and sales by line of business
(4) New capital investment by geographical area and, where applicable, by line of business
(5) A statement of sources and uses of funds
(6) Average number of employees in each geographical area
(7) Research and development expenditure
(8) Transfer pricing policies
(9) Accounting policies used in compiling the published information

Items 1, 2, 4, 6, 7 and 8 on this list fall within the scope of NFI. A comparison with the UN proposals shows that the OECD list is significantly less detailed than the UN's 1977 report, but corresponds more closely to the UN's 1982 report. The authority of these standards is that they are recommendations, and the OECD makes it clear that observance is 'voluntary and not legally enforceable' (OECD, 1976). Unlike the UN proposals, which are aimed at member states, the OECD proposals are aimed directly at MNCs operating in member countries. However, due to the persuasive nature of both sets of proposals, this difference is not considered to be significant. As far as compliance is concerned, the only specific survey performed to date was carried out by the OECD itself (OECD, 1980). However, this survey is concerned with the extent to which the guidelines are included in legal or professional requirements in member countries, rather than with the extent of compliance by MNCs.

In 1978 the OECD Committee on International Investment and Multinational Enterprises established an *ad hoc* working group on accounting standards. The working group's discussions have concentrated on three main themes (Zünd, 1983). The first theme concerns surveys on accounting practices in OECD countries. This includes the 1980 survey referred to above and also a 1981 survey (as yet unpublished) on operating results and segmental information. The second theme concerns clarification of the concepts in the OECD guideline on disclosure of information. The working group has stated its views on new capital investment, average number of employees and research and development expenditure. The third theme concerns future activities of the working group. It does not regard itself as a standard-setting body, but nevertheless intends to work towards promoting the comparability and harmonisation of accounting standards. To this end, it has decided to gather and exchange relevant information, to identify and heighten awareness of the main problem areas and to maintain the momentum for greater harmonisation. A significant recent development is the OECD's plan to hold a summit meeting of the world's leading standard-setting bodies, including private sector and governmental bodies *(International Accounting Bulletin,* 1983c).

The OECD and the UN are therefore both working on the issue of regulating MNCs. Both organisations have published codes of conduct for MNCs, and these codes include the recommendation that MNCs disclose specific NFI. The different sets of proposals reflect the membership and philosophy of the two organisations. The UN standards (particularly the 1977 report) are based on the developing countries' perspective that inward investment may cause more harm than good, and consequently that MNCs need to be subject to extensive controls. However, the OECD recommendations reflect the industrialised environments of its members and are an attempt to promote MNC self-regulation rather than government controls. Although neither set of proposals is mandatory, it would seem that they do reflect a growing demand by interest groups for more information of a non-financial nature, in particular from MNCs operating in developing countries.

14.3.3   The European Economic Community (EEC)

The EEC company law harmonisation programme has had a significant impact on the reporting of financial information, but has had little impact to date on the reporting of non-financial information. Notable exceptions are the Fourth Directive requirements for companies to include in their annual reports and accounts details of employees and details of research and development activities. A significant development is contained in the so-called 'Vredeling initiative', contained in a proposed directive published in 1980. This initiative (named after the individual responsible for its development) would result in companies being required to inform their employees of certain production, investment and employment details (Brown, 1981). This initiative only concerns one particular stakeholder group, namely employees. However, it may indicate the EEC Commission's lack of confidence in the ability of annual reports (in their present format) to satisfy the information needs of interest groups other than shareholders.

14.4   THE AUDIT OF NFI

Chapter 2 discussed the rationale for the auditing of *financial* information. It was suggested that this rationale was based on the accountability of a company's directors to its shareholders, giving rise to the need (and the legal requirement) for the publication of financial information. This information was then given added credibility by the audit function, which was required for the reasons explained under the headings of conflict of interest, consequence, complexity and remoteness. Chapter 2 also referred to agency theory, which proposes that directors themselves benefit from the audit function. This section of Chapter 14 considers whether this rationale should be extended to the audit of non-financial information. It also considers whether auditing *can* be extended in this way. Consequently, the remainder of Chapter 14 discusses first, the desirability of auditing NFI, and secondly, the feasibility of auditing NFI.

14.4.1 Desirability of Auditing NFI

If we accept that the directors of a company are accountable not just to its shareholders but to other interest groups in society, and that this accountability is monitored at least partly through the publication of NFI, then one would expect there to be a demand for the NFI to be given added credibility via the audit process. This demand arises from the same source as the demand for the audit of financial information, namely the following:

- *Conflict of interests*
  User perception of a conflict of interest between preparers and users of NFI would create doubts as to the quality of the NFI produced. Such concern as to possible bias would be reduced if the information was audited by an independent third party

- *Consequence*
  The greater the consequence of the user's decisions (based on the NFI), the greater will be his desire to ensure that the information is of sufficient quality

- *Complexity*
  As the NFI is likely to be as complex as the financial information, one would expect the user to demand that the information be examined by someone of sufficient competence (assuming that the complexity is beyond the grasp of the user himself)

- *Remoteness*
  The user may not have the time or the resources to

examine the information himself. In addition, he may not have the right of access to the information or the underlying subject matter.

The combination of these reasons implies that the users of NFI would create a demand for it to be audited.

In addition, agency theory could be developed as follows to show that directors would also demand an audit of NFI. If directors perceive that society has entrusted them with certain resources only on the condition that such resources are not misused, and if they perceive that society places a higher value on *audited* information concerning those resources, then it is suggested that it is in the directors' own interests to ensure that the NFI is audited.

One of the problems concerning the desirability of auditing NFI lies in assessing a cost-benefit analysis. In the case of shareholders and their relationship to audited financial information, it seems reasonable to suggest that shareholders are willing to bear the costs of the audit (in terms of the auditor's use of management and staff time and the audit fee's impact on profits) in return for the benefits of receiving audited financial information. However, in the case of users of non-financial information, the link between costs and benefits is not so clear (since the costs borne by the company cannot be passed on so directly to those who benefit). Perhaps the neatest solution is to say that although the market cannot establish a *direct* link between the costs and the benefits of auditing NFI, user groups in society *do* bear the costs indirectly through a reduction in the resources which the company has available to use for society's benefit. This assumes that the company is constrained to use its resources in a socially useful way, being thus constrained by the fact that otherwise society will no longer entrust it with the use of these resources.

Finally, the desirability of the audit of NFI can be considered from the viewpoint of the auditor. It seems too superficial to suggest that the auditor would be willing to increase the scope of his audit if this is matched by a similar increase in the size of his fee. The auditing profession prides itself on its status and its reputation for integrity, and it may consider that this reputation could be at risk if the profession moves outside its normal field of competence. Consequently, the auditing profession might be unwilling to risk any damage to its credibility, especially since this loss of credibility may then extend to its reports on *financial* information. From the auditor's viewpoint, the desirability issue is therefore linked to the feasibility issue. If the profession considers itself competent to audit NFI, then one would expect it to be willing to meet the demand for the audit of NFI. The feasibility of auditing NFI is the subject of the next section.

14.4.2 Feasibility of Auditing NFI

The first issue is whether the auditor is competent to examine and report on NFI. One side of the argument is that the auditor's training and experience are concentrated on *financial* matters, and consequently he may not have the necessary skills or expertise to report on non-financial matters. The other side of the argument is that the auditor's existing role already extends beyond financial matters. For example, the auditor must ascertain the existence of stocks and fixed assets as well as their valuation. Also, in the audit of financial statements the auditor often relies on the work of other independent experts in areas outside his field of competence (for example, experts such as chartered surveyors, consultant engineers and actuaries). In addition, in the past the auditor has had to expand his competence in order to deal with changes in the business environment (for example, computer developments) and also with changes in legal requirements (see for example Jack, 1983).

A related issue concerns *who* should audit the NFI. Although the company's auditor may consider himself competent to audit the NFI, there may be other parties who would claim the role of NFI auditor. For example, Sherer and Kent (1983) refer to government-sponsored 'social audits' such as those carried out by the Factory Inspectorate or the Equal Opportunities Commission in the UK. These bodies monitor specific aspects of the social accountability of UK companies. Such government agencies do not deal solely with information published in annual corporate reports. Nevertheless, it could be argued that a government body could best represent the various interest groups concerned with NFI, and consequently that a government body should be responsible for auditing the NFI in company's annual reports. Sherer and Kent also refer to the critical social audits performed by consumer interest groups and other non-shareholder representatives. Again, the scope of these critical social audits extends far beyond the information published in annual financial reports. However, those who perform such audits could argue that they would be more qualified than the auditing profession to perform the audit of the NFI in companies' annual reports.

Another issue arises when the focus is shifted away from the competence of the auditor to the *auditability* of the NFI. This point is discussed in general terms in a background paper prepared by the IFAC Secretariat for the United Nations Commission on Transnational Corporations (United Nations, 1982). The issue can be clarified by considering the type of opinion to be given by the auditor on NFI. The auditor may be competent enough to report on whether the company has complied with the disclosure requirements for individual items of NFI (for example, average number of employees in various categories). However, his opinion would be limited to verifying that the NFI corresponds to the company's records, which in turn reflect the underlying reality of the situation. There is a significant difference in scope between this and the 'true and fair' opinion issued in the UK on the financial information. There are two reasons for this difference. First, there is no requirement for NFI to show a true and fair view (nor is there any similar requirement). Secondly, as Benston (1982) and Perks and Gray (1980) point out, there is no comparable framework of implicit or explicit rules and guidelines influencing the measurements and disclosure of NFI. Until such a framework exists, the auditor cannot issue a 'compliance with generally accepted principles' type of opinion on NFI. Furthermore, until such a framework is placed in an overall context specifying what disclosure of NFI is intended to achieve, the auditor cannot issue a 'true and fair' opinion. Consequently, it seems that in countries where no framework or overall context exists (that is, in most countries), the feasibility of auditing NFI is limited to reporting that the NFI given in the annual report complies with the relevant legislation and is not materially incorrect.

14.5 SUMMARY

This chapter has analysed why the demand for NFI arises, how such demands have been translated into disclosure standards and guidelines by the major supranational organisations, and finally whether the auditing of such information is desirable or feasible. Two main conclusions were drawn from the discussion on the audit of NFI. First, it seems reasonable to suggest that both users and producers of NFI would create a demand for the NFI to be audited. Secondly, a 'true and fair' type of audit is not feasible at present, partly because there is no generally recognised framework of non-financial reporting and partly because there is no accepted consensus as to the overall objective of non-financial reporting.

15 The International Auditing Firms

15.1 INTRODUCTION

A book on international auditing issues would be incomplete without a discussion on the international auditing firms. These firms are described as 'international' for two reasons. First, they are responsible for the audits of most of the world's large MNCs. Secondly, they are represented in most countries of economic significance outside the Eastern bloc. Consequently, the international auditing firms have an important influence on the two main themes running through this book, namely the audit of MNCs and comparative international auditing.

This chapter is organised as follows. Section 15.2 describes the size and nature of the major international auditing firms. Section 15.3 is more analytical, and discusses the firms' differing approaches to matters such as organisation structure and strategies for growth. Finally, Section 15.4 provides a summary and conclusions.

15.2 SIZE AND NATURE OF THE INTERNATIONAL AUDITING FIRMS

A distinction is usually drawn between the 'Big Nine' international auditing firms and the rest. The size of international auditing firms can be measured by a number of

205

206 Other Issues in International Auditing

factors, such a fees, partners, staff, offices or clients. Using almost any definition of size, the smallest of the Big Nine is significantly larger than the next biggest firm. As a result, it seems reasonable to adopt the conventional distinction between the Big Nine and the rest. The Big Nine firms are as follows. (In the rest of this chapter, the firms are referred to by the initials shown in brackets.)

- Arthur Andersen   (AA)
- Arthur Young   (AY)
- Coopers & Lybrand   (C&L)
- Deloitte Haskins & Sells   (DH&S)
- Ernst & Whinney   (E&W)
- Klynveld Main Goerdeler   (KMG)
- Peat Marwick Mitchell   (PMM)
- Price Waterhouse   (PW)
- Touche Ross   (TR)

A smaller 'second division' of four international auditing firms was identified by Bavishi and Wyman (1983). According to one measure of size, namely clients' sales and assets, if these four firms combined they would still be smaller than the smallest of the Big Nine. This emphasises the extent of the gap in size between the Big Nine firms and the other international firms. The four firms referred to above are as follows:

- Binder Dijker Otte   (BDO)
- Fox Moore International   (FMI)
- Grant Thornton International   (GTI)
- Horwath and Horwath International   (HHI)

The 'Big Thirteen' refers to the Big Nine plus these four firms.

An analysis of the operations and results of the Big Nine firms is hampered by the relative scarcity of publicly available data. Compared to the MNCs that they audit, the Big Nine firms disclose significantly less information on their financial position and performance. The main reason for this is that auditing firms are normally organised in the form of partnerships, and so are subject to few (if any) disclosure requirements. In a partnership, unlike a large limited company, there is (theoretically at least) no separation of ownership and control. Consequently, the 'owners' of the auditing firm can obtain financial information about the firm from *internal* sources, and so there is less need to produce external financial reports. Proponents of the accountability argument (see Chapter 2) could argue that the auditing firms are accountable and so should report, not only to the owners, but also to other interest groups in society such as employees, creditors, lenders, the government and the general public. The annual external reports published by some of the Big Nine since the late 1970s could represent a response to this perceived demand for information from a variety of interest groups.

From a user perspective, there are several disadvantages of such voluntary disclosure. First, the information presented is selective in nature, in that the auditing firm may only disclose the positive aspects of its operations. Secondly, there is no generally accepted framework of measurement and disclosure rules against which users can measure the quality and quantity of the information disclosed. Thirdly, the information is not subject to audit, and so lacks the 'added credibility' that the audit profession is normally considered to provide to company financial reports. The supply of these voluntary disclosures has diminished in the early 1980s.

Some of the Big Nine firms have been reluctant to publish detailed information. This seems to be partly because they do not consider the data to be particularly meaningful, and partly because they consider that professional firms should be measured in terms of quality of service rather than in terms of size.

There are other sources of publicly available information

on the Big Nine firms apart from their voluntary financial reports. For example, all the Big Nine firms publish directories that list details of offices, countries and partners. Bavishi and Wyman (1983) have undertaken a major analysis of company financial reports in order to determine the auditors of over 10 000 leading companies worldwide. They used this database to determine the type, size and geographical spread of clients of the Big Nine firms. In some countries, notably the UK, Australia and South Africa, companies are required to disclose their audit fee in their annual financial statements. This is a useful information source for determining the size and significance of auditing firms. However, because only a few countries require this disclosure, the information cannot be gathered on a total worldwide basis.

The international auditing firms may also disclose data to specific interest groups but not to the general public. This disclosure may be done on a voluntary basis or it may be required by law. For example, the Big Nine firms may disclose to their staff financial statistics that are not publicly available. The firms may need to disclose confidential financial information to banks in order to obtain overdraft facilities. In some countries, auditing firms are required by law to provide statistics on individual audit assignments. In Japan, for example, audit firms are required to supply the government with details of staff and of time spent per audit area for each audit client.

Of the financial information that the Big Nine firms make publicly available, total fee income is the statistic that is most commonly disclosed and that seems to generate most interest. Profit figures are rarely disclosed, partly because of an unwillingness to disclose what is perceived to be sensitive information, and partly because of the difficulty in distinguishing between the 'salary' element, the 'return on capital' element and the residual 'profit' element of partnership profits. Comparisons of total fee income are hindered by the fact that the Big Nine firms do not all have the same financial year. Also, most comparisons are based on dollar figures, which may not be particularly meaningful to a firm such as KMG that earns most of its fee income outside the US. Rentoul (1982) refers to allegations by some firms that other firms are 'double counting' and are using different bases for measuring fee income. An example of different measurement bases is the use by some firms of a cash basis and the use by other firms of an accruals basis. The *International Accounting Bulletin* (1983d) published a league table based on 1983 fee income (31 December 1982 in the case of AY). This gave the following ranking:

		1983 *$m*
(1)	Arthur Andersen	1238
(2)	Peat Marwick Mitchell	1230
(3)	Coopers & Lybrand	1100
(4)	Price Waterhouse	1013
(5)	Klynveld Main Goerdeler	1000
(6)	Ernst & Whinney	972
(7)	Arthur Young	955
(8)	Deloitte Haskins & Sells	900
(9)	Touche Ross	(refused to disclose)

Accountancy Age published a league table based on 1982 fee income (Rentoul, 1983). This table attempted to solve the problem of differing year ends by extrapolating the financial year's total of each firm at 1 per cent per calendar month up to December 1982. This produced the following ranking:

		1982 *$m*
(1)	Peat Marwick Mitchell	1219
(2)	Arthur Andersen	1168

(3)	Coopers & Lybrand	1098
(4)	Price Waterhouse	1003
(5)	Arthur Young	977
(6)	KMG	970
(7)	Deloitte Haskins & Sells	920
(8)	Ernst & Whinney	914
(9)	Touche Ross	832

Bavishi and Wyman (1983) produce the following ranking of the Big Nine in terms of 1981 worldwide revenues:

		1981 *$m*
(1)	Coopers & Lybrand	998
(2)	Peat Marwick Mitchell	979
(3)	Arthur Andersen	973
(4)	Klynveld Main Goerdeler	850
(5)	Price Waterhouse	850
(6)	Deloitte Haskins & Sells	800
(7)	Arthur Young	750
(8)	Ernst & Whinney	706
(9)	Touche Ross	700

Bavishi and Wyman also collected data on other size criteria, such as number of partners, number of offices and size of audit clients (measured by sales and assets of clients companies). Measurement of the Big Nine against these criteria produces a variety of rankings, as shown in Table 15.1.

The Big Nine domination is broken up in the 'Offices' category. Grant Thornton International have more offices than AY and AA, and Binder Dijker Otte have more offices than AA. However, in all the other categories there is a significant gap between the lowest-ranked Big Nine firm and the next largest firm.

These global figures and rankings mask significant differences at the regional level. Firms that are in the top four in a

TABLE 15.1 *Ranking of the Big Nine worldwide according to various size criteria*

Income	Partners	Offices	Client Sales	Client Assets
C&L	KMG	C&L	PW	PW
PMM	C&L	DH&S	C&L	PMM
AA	PMM	TR	DH&S	DH&S
KMG	DH&S	KMG	AA	C&L
PW	TR	PW	AY	AY
DH&S	AY	PMM	KMG	KMG
AY	PW	E&W	PMM	E&W
E&W	E&W	AY	E&W	TR
TR	AA	AA	TR	AA

SOURCE: Based on information in Bavishi and Wyman, 1983.

global ranking may be near the foot of a particular regional ranking. Bavishi and Wyman calculated the regional distribution of Big Nine clients (according to location of sales and assets audited), and their statistics reveal several interesting regional differences. For example, 86 per cent of AA's client sales and assets are in North America, compared to only 10 per cent for KMG. 34 per cent of TR's client sales and assets are in the Asia/Pacific region, compared to only 3 per cent for C&L. 79 per cent of KMG's client sales and assets are in Europe, compared to only 16 per cent for PMM.

These regional differences can be highlighted by comparing league tables for the US and the UK. These tables show, for example, that AA, the number one firm in the US (measured by fee income), is number nine in the UK, and that DH&S, the number two firm in the UK, is number eight in the US. The most recent comparative data for the national firms of the Big Nine is given in Table 15.2.

In the UK, Thornton Baker (part of GTI) comes in above both AA and KMG, with fee income of £40m. According to the 'Top 20' table in the *Financial Times* (1983), the biggest

TABLE 15.2 *Fee income of the Big Nine in the UK and the US*

	UK Fees £m		US Fees $m
PMM	64.3	AA	909
DH&S	60.5	PMM	750
PW	60.2	C&L	625
C&L	60	E&W	625
E&W	52	PW	493
TR	48	AY	440
AY	46	TR	420
AA	35	DH&S	415
KMG	31.6	KMG	179

SOURCE: *Financial Times* (1983) and Savage (1983b).

gap in the UK is between the firms ranked 13 and 14. Consequently, the UK seems to have a 'Big Thirteen' rather than a Big Nine set of leading firms. The other firms in the top thirteen are Binder Hamlyn (part of BDO), Spicer and Pegler, and Pannell Kerr Forster. There is also a significant gap between the firms ranked 4 and 5 in the UK, and so for some purposes it would seem reasonable to talk of the 'Big Four' in the UK. In the US, there is a more obvious gap between the biggest firms and the rest, as the ninth largest firm is less than half the size of the eighth largest. This explains why the Big Eight is a more common term in the US than the Big Nine.

Comparative fee income data is not available for regional areas such as Europe. However, Bavishi and Wyman provide data on number of partners and offices by regions, and this leads to the rankings of the Big Nine shown in Table 15.3. BDO and GTI would appear sixth and seventh respectively in the ranking by partners, and would appear sixth and fifth respectively in the ranking by offices.

These regional differences can influence the structure and

TABLE 15.3 *Ranking of the Big Nine in Europe according to total partners and total offices*

Partners	Offices
KMG	KMG
DH&S	DH&S
C&L	C&L
AY	TR
TR	AY
PW	PW
PMM	PMM
E&W	E&W
AA	AA

SOURCE: Based on information in Bavishi and Wyman, 1983.

strategies of the Big Nine firms. For example, a firm such as Arthur Andersen may find it relatively easy to operate a highly centralised organisational structure, when a high percentage of their global operations is concentrated in one particular geographical area. Some Big Nine firms are fairly loose groupings of national firms with strong local identities. In these cases, the national firms may be more concerned with size statistics on a national rather than global basis. Also, the power and influence of the different national firms in the internal management of a Big Nine firm may depend not just on absolute size (measured by national fee income), but on relative size (measured by national *ranking* of fee income). Comparative structures and strategies is the subject of the next section.

15.3 ANALYSIS OF STRUCTURES AND STRATEGIES

The structures and strategies of the Big Nine firms are two important inter-relating factors to be considered when analysing the nature and development of these firms. Organisation structure will influence a firm's ability to respond to national and international opportunities. Conversely, the strategies by which a firm has grown in the past will affect the organisation structure of the international firm.

There are considerable differences in the organisational structure of the Big Nine firms. These differences are apparent from the firm-by-firm descriptions in sources such as Rentoul (1982) and *International Accounting Bulletin* (1983b). Weinstein *et al.* (1978) adopt a more analytical approach, and provide five models of organisational structure employed by international accounting firms. Bavishi and Wyman (1983) provide a statistical analysis of the office/partner directories of the international auditing firms. Perceptions of organisation structures are confused by the differing attitudes of the Big Nine in different situations. For example, if a firm is trying to gain (or hold on to) the audit of a large MNC, it would portray itself as a single worldwide firm with consistent standards of client service. However, if the same firm were tendering for a government contract, it might emphasise its strong national identity and play down its international links.

The situation is complicated further by the difference between the organisation structure and the actual legal structure of the international firms. The legal structure is particularly relevant in the case of lawsuits such as that reported by Krijgsman (1982) involving AM International and Price Waterhouse. Lawyers acting for the shareholders of AM International, a US company, have filed a suit against not only the PW partnership in the US but also the PW partnerships in a number of other countries. It is likely that most Big Nine firms, if faced with a similar lawsuit, would argue that each national partnership is autonomous and that the 'international' organisation is only an administrative arrangement for sharing certain common costs. The legal definition of an 'international firm' has still to be provided by the courts.

Weinstein *et al.* (1978) claim that their set of five organisational models captures the essence of the various structures adopted by the international auditing firms. The study predates the founding of KMG, and consequently only deals with the Big Eight. Weinstein *et al.*'s Model 1 is a US partnership with centralised control. Individual offices are profit centres for management and control purposes, but profits are shared on an international rather than a national basis. Model 2 results from a large US firm and a large UK firm joining their names and becoming known internationally as one firm. The European partnership is largely autonomous from the UK and US firms. Partnership profits are shared on a national basis. Model 3 is similar to Model 2, but in this case both the UK and the US firms have a significant equity interest in the European partnership. The remaining equity interest is held by the individual European offices. Model 4 is more diverse and opportunistic. Some European offices are owned by European headquarters and some are owned by a combination of the US and UK partnerships. Some European offices may only be correspondent firms. Model 5 is a grouping of individual national partnerships who form a correspondent relationship overseen by an international federation.

The principal distinguishing feature of each model seems to be the degree of centralised control. The extent of centralised control may have a positive or negative impact on a firm's performance. For example, a high degree of centralisation may make it easier for the firm to present a uniform image worldwide and to maintain consistent standards of quality control. A low degree of centralisation may permit the individual national firms to adapt more quickly to changes in the local business environment.

Although Weinstein *et al.* clearly had specific firms in mind when constructing their models, they do not name the firms in each model. An attempt to allocate the Big Nine firms to the five models reveals the weaknesses of their categorisation. Although Arthur Andersen and KMG clearly fit into Models 1 and 5 respectively, the occupants of Models 2, 3 and 4 are less obvious. Weinstein *et al.* seem to imply that Deloitte Haskins & Sells and Ernst & Whinney belong in Model 2. However, both these firms have some of the characteristics of Model 4. Price Waterhouse has adopted the policy of making each partner in its individual offices a partner in PW's world firm, in contrast to the more usual arrangement whereby the national firms are members of the international firm. PW's arrangement shows characteristics of the 'world partnership' concept embodied in Model 1. However, PW actually describes its structure as federal, which comes under Model 5 (Rentoul, 1982). The other firms could all be allocated to Model 3, with varying degrees of overlap with Models 2 and 4.

Weinstein *et al.* restricted the scope of their study by focusing on the European operations of the international firms. Consequently, they ignore the particular characteristics of the sizeable accounting market in the Far East. In the Philippines, for example, the accounting market is dominated by one firm, SyCip Gorres Velayo (SGV), which has affiliations with four of the Big Nine firms (Bavishi and Wyman, 1983). The study also ignores the South American and African operations of the Big Nine firms. However, despite its limitations, the study is a useful attempt at classifying the identifying features of the differing organisational structures of the international firms.

Bavishi and Wyman (1983) approached the structure issue on a national rather than an international level. They identified seven categories of organisational structure used in individual countries. Their analysis was based on the office/partner directories produced by the international firms. The seven categories are as follows:

(1) International name
(2) Combined name
(3) Local name
(4) Association
(5) Correspondent
(6) Multiple affiliations
(7) Two plus names

Category 2 refers to cases where a firm uses a combined local and international name in a particular country. Category 6 refers to firms such as SGV (mentioned previously) which are affiliated to more than one Big Nine firm. Category 7 refers to instances where an international firm practises under two or more local firms' names in one particular country. There are similarities between this set of seven categories and Weinstein *et al.*'s five models. For example, an international firm that always operated under Category 1 would seem to fall into Model 1. Category 4 and Model 5 seem similar. Category 5 could fall into Models 4 or 5. The distinctions between the seven categories are not always clear. For example, Category 4 was established specifically to cater for federations such as KMG. However, member firms of KMG could be considered to fall into Category 2, as they often use their own local name in combination with the KMG name.

Bavishi and Wyman's analysis of the firm directories revealed several interesting statistics. Four of the Big Nine adopted Category 1 (international name) for nearly all their partners. These four firms are AA, E&W, PMM and PW, all of which used Category 1 for around 90 per cent or more of their total partners. Another two firms, C&L and DH&S, used Category 1 for around 75 per cent of their total partners. The firm with the highest percentage in Category 3 (local firm) was TR, with a figure of 33 per cent. The firm with the highest percentage in Category 7 (two plus names) was AY, with a figure of 39 per cent. All of KMG's partners came under Category 4 (association). The analysis of organisation structure by region showed several differences, reflecting to some extent the regional strengths of the particular Big Nine firms. In the US, 82 per cent of the Big Thirteen partners practise under an international name, compared to 42 per cent in non-US countries. In Europe, almost as many Big Thirteen partners practise under an association as under an international name (32 per cent against 34 per cent).

The preceding paragraphs have analysed the international auditing firms in terms of their organisational structures. These structures affect, and also reflect, the strategies that these firms adopt to increase their international coverage. However, before analysing how the Big Nine internationalise their operations, it would seem useful to consider *why* they do this.

The motives of an international auditing firm can be compared to, and contrasted with, those of an MNC. Traditional economic theory suggests that the primary objective of a limited company is to maximise the return to its shareholders (in net present value terms). This can be termed the goal of profit maximisation. An alternative view is provided by emphasising the separation of ownership and control of the large modern company. This separation may permit the directors and managers of the company to pursue goals that conflict with profit maximisation. For example, the directors and managers may seek to maximise their own salaries, status or security at the expense of the shareholders. However, the shareholders may be able to constrain the actions of management in such a way that the two sets of goals are congruent. There are a number of theories that attempt to explain why a uninational company decides to internationalise its operations and undertake foreign direct investment (FDI). One explanation of FDI is given by the 'product life-cycle model' (Hood and Young, 1979). This theory suggests that there is no incentive to undertake FDI until a company has passed the development stage of a new product and is entering the maturing stage, by which time its national competitors have caught up with the innovation and have narrowed domestic profit margins. Calvet (1981) examines two facets of the foreign expansion of companies. One is the foreign involvement, which arises due to company-specific and country-specific factors. The other is the internationalisation within the MNC. Such internationalisation arises in response to the organisational difficulties in establishing satisfactory contractual agreements.

This brief summary of the motives of an MNC provides a background against which to view the motives of an international auditing firm. There are several differences between the two types of organisations. First, an auditing firm provides a service, whereas a typical MNC produces goods. Buckley and O'Sullivan (1981) refer to four differences between service products (such as audits) and manufacturing products. These four differences are intangibility, perishability, heterogeneity and simultaneity. Services are intangible and so a prospective purchaser has relatively little evidence on which to base an assessment of the service product's quality. Consequently, the reputation of the service firm is an important factor in influencing the prospective purchaser's decision. Services are perishable, and so a service firm cannot build up 'stocks' of service products when demand fluctuates. This affects the staffing policies of the auditing firms, and also provides an incentive for them to expand their non-cyclical services such as tax and consultancy work. Service products are heterogeneous, and consequently the quality of an audit may vary over time or between offices. Consequently, quality control is particularly important for service firms. Service products are generally simultaneous, in that production and consumption occurs at the same time. This affects the location of the providers of audit services. Although perishability and simultaneity overlap to some extent, the above analysis does help to clarify some of the differences between service products and manufacturing products.

A second difference between international auditing firms and MNCs is that auditing is a profession. One of the distinguishing features of a profession is that its members would claim to place their clients' interests above their own interests. Benson (1981) considers that the primary responsibility of a member of a profession is to serve his clients. If this is accepted, then the main objective of an auditing firm would not be profit maximisation. This is not to say that auditors are not high earners. However, auditors could justify their rewards by reference to the substantial risks they face (particularly that of unlimited liability), and also by reference to the lengthy period of education and training that is required. Also, although profit maximisation may not be an auditing firm's main objective, this does not preclude profit maximising behaviour on the part of the auditing firm. For example, such behaviour might only occur at certain times, and might cease when it creates a conflict with the perceived client service objective. Profit maximising behaviour might occur as a direct result of pursuing the client service objective (for example, reduction of unnecessary costs). However, although auditing firms may indulge in profit maximising behaviour, it seems likely that their primary objective would be stated in terms of client service rather than profit maximisation.

A third difference between international auditing firms and MNCs is that auditing firms are generally partnerships rather than limited liability companies. The partners of a Big Nine firm are the 'owners' of the local, national or international firm (depending on the organisational structure). In theory, there is no separation of ownership and control in a partnership, as there is likely to be in a large MNC. In practice, however, control of a partnership may be concentrated in the hands of a relatively small number of senior partners. Another implication of a partnership structure is that the partners generally have unlimited liability (unlike the owners and managers of most MNCs). This is likely to affect the partners' attitude to risk. The implications of unlimited liability may not be significant if the partners are covered by a professional indemnity policy. However, such insurance policies nearly always specify an upper limit to the cover they provide, in which case the partners would ultimately have unlimited liability.

An international auditing firm differs from an MNC not only in the nature of its organisation, but also in its motives for internationalisation. Wu and Hackett (1977) analysed the factors motivating US accounting firms to expand into foreign markets. They found that the most important factors were the desire to serve current clients moving into particular foreign markets and the desire to prevent erosion of current client/firm relationships. Factors such as return on investment, impact on financial statements and saturation of the US market were ranked as being relatively unimportant. It is likely that an MNC would consider these three factors to be significantly more important in determining whether, and where, to internationalise. Wu and Hackett suggested that the motives for internationalisation could be grouped into three distinct categories, namely client service, defensive management strategy and offensive management strategy. Client service was considered to be the most important, and offensive management strategy the least important. The pre-eminence of client service is emphasised by Macrae (1981), who considered client service to be the key factor in the historical development of the international operations of UK and US accounting firms. Wu and Hackett's study has certain limitations. They analyse the international firms purely from a US perspective, and so do not attempt to explain the motives of European-based firms such as KMG. Their study is based on responses from the international firms. As in the case of any individual or group, stated motives may differ from implicit motives. Finally, their study was performed in the mid-1970s, since when the international firms seem to have adopted an increasingly commercial and business-orientated approach.

The preceding paragraphs have analysed why the international auditing firms expand their international operations. The remainder of this section deals with *how* they expand their international operations. There are a number of internationalisation strategies that can be adopted. An international firm may establish a correspondent relationship with an existing local firm. The international firm would normally use only one correspondent firm per country. However, that local firm may act as correspondent to more than one international firm. An existing local firm may become a member of the international firm, or, depending on the structure of the international firm, the partners in the existing local firm may become partners in the international firm. This arrangement is effectively a merger or takeover, and may involve partners in the international firm moving into the new member firm. An international firm may establish a new practice in a country where it has not previously been represented. Finally, an international firm may form a joint venture with an existing local practice. The international firm may have a majority interest, an equal interest or a minority interest in the joint venture.

The internationalisation strategy of a particular firm is influenced by its existing worldwide organisational structure. If a firm is one worldwide partnership with centralised control (Weinstein *et al.*'s Model 1), then that firm is likely to want close control over any additions to the international firm. Consequently, such a firm would be unlikely to enter into a correspondent relationship with national firms in new foreign markets. Instead, it would probably establish a new office in that particular country, and staff that office with mainly expatriate partners and managers. Alternatively, it might merge with, or take over, an existing local practice, preferably on the basis that partners from the international firm have effective management control of the combined practice. If Wu and Hackett's analysis is correct, and client service is the primary motive for internationalisation, then the above 'expatriate office' concept is likely to be an effective strategy. This is because the new office will be concerned mainly with servicing the overseas operations of existing MNC clients, and consequently will have substantial contact with expatriates in the overseas subsidiary and/or with management from the MNC parent company. However, if the primary motive for internationalisation is not client service but an offensive management strategy, then the 'expatriate office' concept may be adapted to incorporate a significant number of *local* partners and managers to attract and service new local clients.

At the other end of the organisational structures range is a firm that is a federation of correspondents (Weinstein *et al.*'s Model 5). Such a firm would tend to expand its international operations by forming new correspondent relationships in countries where it was not previously represented. It seems unlikely that such a firm would merge with, or take over, an existing local firm, nor does it seem likely that it would establish a completely new practice in a new foreign market. The internationalisation strategy of such a firm would seem to be motivated by the desire to serve current clients who have moved into new foreign markets, rather than by offensive management considerations.

Wu and Hackett (1977) ranked the strategies used most frequently by US accounting firms when entering new foreign markets. This ranking was based on the responses of the firms themselves. The forming of agency or correspondent relationships was easily the most popular strategy, and there was little difference between the popularity of the other strategies. Wu and Hackett's ranking of strategies is subject to the limitations mentioned earlier, namely that it is based solely on a US perspective, it assumes that stated strategies are identical to actual strategies and it may have been overtaken by changes in the international environment since the mid-1970s.

The advantages and disadvantages of the main internationalisation strategies can be summarised as follows. The advantages of a correspondent relationship are its relatively low cost and its flexibility. However, the international firm may have difficulties in establishing and maintaining uniform standards of client service. Mergers and takeovers provide an established local client base, but they can be difficult to back out of if the international firm considers subsequently that it made the wrong decision. Starting a new local office from scratch has the advantage of allowing greater head office control and of being able to rely on partners and managers who have proven ability within the international firm. However, there may be difficulties in establishing a new national identity and in attracting new local clients.

15.4   SUMMARY

This chapter began by providing various statistics relating to the international auditing firms. There are no legal requirements for these firms to disclose financial or non-financial information. The voluntary disclosures made are concerned mainly with fee income and with non-financial data such as numbers of offices, partners and staff. Consequently, a comparative analysis normally concentrates on size criteria rather than efficiency or profitability criteria. In the case of a professional firm, quality of service may be a more meaningful yardstick than absolute size (as measured by fee income). However, quality of service is not easily measured and does not feature in the league tables of the international firms. Section 15.3 then discussed the various organisation structures adopted by the international auditing firms. This section also analysed the motives for internationalisation, and contrasted these motives with those of an MNC. Finally, the methods of internationalisation were analysed, and were related to the various organisational structures described earlier.

Part IV
Concluding Remarks

16   Summary and Conclusions

The preceding chapters have examined a number of key issues in international auditing. Chapter 1 established why the topic of international auditing was worthy of study. Chapter 2 provided some background to the subsequent chapters by analysing why there is a need for auditing and auditing standards. The discussion was placed in an international context by analysing the particular relevance of auditing and auditing standards to MNCs.

Chapters 3 to 10 outlined the auditing standards in eight countries. Each of these chapters started by describing the key features of the country's auditing and accounting environment. That environment is an important influence on the development of national auditing standards. Each chapter then described first, the source, history and authority; and secondly, the scope and content, of the country's auditing standards. In some countries, such as Germany and Japan, some or all of the auditing standards are issued by a quasi-governmental body, whereas in other countries the accounting profession is the source of the auditing standards. The Netherlands does not have a set of codified auditing standards as such, but has a number of professional pronouncements that carry a substantial degree of authority.

There are significant differences in the history of the auditing standards in the countries studied. For example, the United States has had codified auditing standards for several decades. Countries such as Japan and the United Kingdom have only recently introduced codified auditing standards. However, the United Kingdom, unlike Japan, has a well-established accounting profession with a history of uncodified auditing standards. The authority of the auditing standards is usually mandatory in the countries studied, and the source of the authority normally depends on the source of the auditing standards. However, in Canada the auditing standards are issued by the profession but have legal authority.

The scope of the auditing standards generally includes all occasions when an audit is performed. However, the BADC auditing standards in Japan only apply to the independent audits under the Securities and Exchange Law, which governs the financial statements of publicly traded companies. Contents of auditing standards usually consist of personal standards, performance standards and reporting standards. In some of the countries studied some personal standards were excluded from the set of codified auditing standards but were included in other professional pronouncements. For example, in the UK standards of independence are included in the ethical guides of the professional bodies. Reporting standards are influenced to some extent by company law, but normally include a requirement for a 'true and fair' or 'present fairly' type of opinion and sometimes also include a 'compliance with the law' opinion. The German standards require only a 'compliance with the law' opinion.

Any international comparison of auditing standards must take into account the differences in auditing and accounting environments around the world. Chapters 3 to 10 show the environmental differences that exist in eight developed countries. Such environmental differences lead to differences in auditing standards and also to differing interpretations of apparently similar auditing standards. For example, national interpretations of auditor independence and of 'true and fair' may differ depending on the particular legal and business culture. Chapters 3 to 10 attempt to show not only the differences and similarities in national auditing standards but also the differences and similarities in the underlying environments.

Chapters 11 to 15 dealt with a number of other issues in international auditing. Chapters 11 and 12 considered the problems that arise in the audits of MNCs. These chapters focused on audit problems that are peculiar to MNCs, and did not consider in any detail those audit problems that are common to both MNCs and large uninational companies. In general, the main audit problems in MNCs arise from international differences in auditing and accounting environments, such as for example the differences apparent in Chapter 3 to 10. These problems may be magnified when the MNC operates in countries where there are no established auditing standards.

Chapter 13 considered the issue of harmonisation. International harmonisation of auditing standards seems to be a possible solution to the problems discussed in the previous two chapters. International harmonisation is also considered to provide benefits to a user of non-domestic financial statements, as harmonisation is considered to facilitate the international comparison of financial statements. Chapter 13 discussed the theoretical and practical barriers to progress in international harmonisation. It also analysed the current influences on harmonisation, and explained the objectives (and the limitations) of the International Federation of Accountants.

Chapter 14 dealt with an emerging issue in international auditing, namely the audit of non-financial information (NFI). Although it seems likely that users of NFI would create a demand for the audit of NFI, there are difficulties in performing a 'true and fair' type of audit on NFI. This is because there is at present no generally accepted framework of objectives and rules for the reporting of NFI.

Chapter 15 described the size and nature of the international auditing firms, and analysed their structures and strategies. Although there is a substantial body of literature on why and how MNCs expand their international operations, remarkably little has been written on the auditing firms. This chapter reviewed the current literature and compared and contrasted the motives of MNCs and audit firms. One significant difference is the auditing firms' client service motive. This may over-ride the profit motive, and can affect the internationalisation strategies of the auditing firms.

There are a number of areas in international auditing where further research could be useful and also interesting. For example, there is scope for further research into comparative international auditing. The analysis in Part II could be applied to other industrialised countries and also to less-developed countries. The practical experience developed by the international auditing firms in the audit of MNCs provides a fund of knowledge that could form the basis of further research into the problems detailed in Chapters 11 and 12. There is scope for further research into the harmonisation issue, for example to assess the success of IFAC by measuring the extent to which IFAC's international auditing guidelines have been incorporated into the codified auditing standards of its member bodies. Research could be carried out into the nature and extent of the demand for the audit of non-financial information. Such research could test the hypothesis proposed in Chapter 14 that a demand for the audit of NFI would arise for basically the same reasons as the demand for the audit of financial information. Finally, there is scope for research into the effects of the strategies of the international auditing firms.

References

Accountants' International Study Group (1969) 'Using the Work and Report of Another Auditor' (Toronto: AISG).

Accountant's Magazine (1980a) 'Policing Auditing Standards', *The Accountant's Magazine*, January, pp. 4–5.

Accountant's Magazine (1980b) 'Rules for Auditors' (editorial), *The Accountant's Magazine*, May, p. 180.

American Accounting Association (1973) *A Statement of Basic Auditing Concepts*, Committee on Basic Auditing Concepts (Studies in Accounting Research no. 6) (Sarasota, Florida: AAA).

American Institute of Certified Public Accountants (1972) *Part of Examination made by Other Independent Auditors* (AICPA Professional Standards, AU s543) (New York: AICPA).

American Institute of Certified Public Accountants (1975) *Professional Accounting in 30 Countries* (New York: AICPA).

American Institute of Certified Public Accountants (1978) *Report of the Commission on Auditors' Responsibilities* (The Cohen Commission) (New York: AICPA).

American Institute of Certified Public Accountants (1983) *AICPA Professional Standards (Volumes A and B)* (New York: AICPA).

Anderson, R.J. (1977) *The External Audit* (Toronto: Copp Clark Pitman).

Arens, A.A. and J.K. Loebbecke (1976) *Auditing: An Integrated Approach* (Englewood Cliffs, New Jersey: Prentice-Hall).

Arpan, J.S. and L.H. Radebaugh (1981) *International Accounting and Multinational Enterprises* (Boston, Mass.: Warren, Gorham and Lamont).

Auditing Practices Committee (1976) *'True and Fair'*, Issue no. 1, Autumn.

233

Auditing Practices Committee (1978) *Auditing Standards and Guidelines: Discussion Drafts* (London: APC).

Ball, R., R.G. Walker and G.P. Whittred (1979) 'Audit Qualifications and Share Prices', *Abacus,* June, pp. 23–34.

Bartholomew, E.G. (1978) 'The EEC and Auditors' Qualifications', *The Accountant's Magazine,* August, pp. 333–5.

Bavishi, V.B. and H.E. Wyman (1983) *Who Audits the World* (Storrs, Connecticut: Centre for Transnational Accounting and Financial Research).

Beeny, J.H. (1975) *European Financial Reporting: West Germany* (London: ICAEW).

Beeny, J.H. (1976) *European Financial Reporting: France* (London: ICAEW).

Beeny, J.H. and J.G. Chastney (1978) *European Financial Reporting: The Netherlands* (London: ICAEW).

Benson, H. (1981) 'Standards: The Hallmark of a Profession', *The Journal of Accountancy,* February, pp. 45–8.

Benston, G.J. (1976) *Corporate Financial Disclosure in the UK and the USA* (Farnborough: Saxon House).

Benston, G.J. (1979/80) 'The Market for Public Accounting Services: Demand, Supply and Regulation' *The Accounting Journal,* vol. 2, pp. 2–46.

Benston, G.J. (1982) 'Accounting and Corporate Accountability', *Accounting, Organisations and Society,* vol. 7, no. 2, pp. 87–105.

Black, A.D. and A.M. Eastwood (1980) 'Audit Evidence – The Benefits of Monetary Unit Sampling', *The Accountant's Magazine,* May, pp. 197–200.

Brennan, J.W. (ed.) (1979) *The Internationalisation of the Accountancy Profession* (Toronto: CICA).

Bromwich, M., A.G. Hopwood and J. Shaw (eds) (1982) *Auditing Research: Issues and Opportunities* (London: Deloitte Haskins & Sells).

Bromwich, M. and A.G. Hopwood (eds) (1983) *Accounting Standards Setting: An International Perspective* (London: Pitman).

Brown, A (1981) 'Social (R)evolution in the EEC', *The Accountant's Magazine,* March, pp. 83–4.

Buckley, J.W. and P.R. O'Sullivan (1981) 'International Economics and Multinational Accounting Firms' in J.C. Burton (ed.), *The International World of Accounting: Challenges and Opportunities* (Reston, Virginia: The Council of Arthur Young Professors).

Burton J.C. (ed.) (1981) *The International World of Accounting: Challenges and Opportunities* (1980 Proceedings of the Arthur Young Professors' Round Table) (Reston, Virginia: The Council of Arthur Young Professors).

Calvet, A.L. (1981) 'A Synthesis of Foreign Direct Investment Theories and Theories of the Multinational Firm', *Journal of International Business Studies,* Spring/Summer, pp. 43–59.

Campbell, L.G. (1983) 'Current accounting practices in Japan', *The Accountant's Magazine,* August, pp. 303–6.

Canadian Institute of Chartered Accountants (1978) *Report of the Special Committee to Examine the Role of the Auditor* (The Adams Committee) (Toronto: CICA).

Carsberg, B. and A. Eastergard (1981) 'Financial Reporting in North America', in Nobes and Parker, *Comparative International Accounting* (Oxford: Philip Allan), pp. 9–34.

Chastney, J.G. (1975) *True and Fair View* (London: ICAEW).

Chetkovich, M.N. (1979) 'The International Federation of Accountants: Its Organization and Goals', *International Journal of Accounting,* vol. 15, no. 1, pp. 13–20.

Chow, C.W. and S.J. Rice (1982a) 'Qualified Auditor Opinions and Auditor Switching', *The Accounting Review,* April, pp. 326–35.

Chow, C.W. and S.J. Rice (1982b) 'Qualified Audit Opinions and Share Prices – An Investigation', *Auditing – A Journal of Theory and Practice,* Winter, pp. 35–53.

Collins, L. and D. Pham (1983) 'Research into the Processes of Accounting Standards Setting in France,' in Bromwich and Hopwood, *Accounting Standards Setting: An International Perspective* (London: Pitman), pp. 71–86.

Compagnie Nationale des Commissaires aux Comptes (1980) *Recommendations Relatives A L'Exercise des Missions* (Paris: CNCC).

CTC Reporter (1983) 'Report of the *Ad Hoc* Working Group', *CTC Reporter,* Winter, pp. 18–21.

Deloitte Haskins & Sells (1980) *Corporate Reporting and*

Accounting Practices in France (Paris: Deloitte Haskins & Sells).

Dierkes, M. (1979) 'Corporate Social Reporting in Germany: Conceptual Developments and Practical Experience' *Accounting, Organizations and Society,* vol. 4, no. 1/2, pp. 87–107.

Dunning, J.H. (ed.) (1974) *Economic Analysis and the Multinational Enterprise* (New York: Praeger).

Dykxhoorn, H.J. and K.E. Sinning (1981) 'The Independence Issue Concerning German Auditors: A Synthesis', *International Journal of Accounting,* vol. 16, no. 2, Spring, pp. 163–81.

Eiteman, D.K. and A.I. Stonehill (1982) *Multinational Business Finance* (3rd edn) (Reading, Mass: Addison-Wesley).

Estes, R. and M. Reimer (1977) 'A Study of the Effect of Qualified Auditors' Opinions on Bankers' Lending Decisions', *Accounting and Business Research,* Autumn, pp. 250–9.

Estes, R. and M. Reimer (1979) 'An Experimental Study of the Differential Effect of Standard and Qualified Auditors' Opinions on Investors' Price Decisions', *Accounting and Business Research,* Spring, pp. 157–62.

Financial Times (1983) 'Accountancy', *Financial Times,* 8 November, pp. 23–6.

Firth, M. (1978) 'Qualified Audit Reports: Their Impact on Investment Decisions', *The Accounting Review,* July, pp. 642–50.

Firth, M. (1980) 'Perceptions of Auditor Independence and Official Ethical Guidelines', *The Accounting Review,* July, pp. 451–66.

Flint, D. (1980) *Auditing Standards: Purpose, Authority and Quality Control* (New South Wales: Australian Society of Accountants, (NSW Division).

Flint, D. (1982) 'Social and Ethical Issues in Auditing' in Bromwich, Hopwood and Shaw, *Auditing Research: Issues and Opportunities* (London: Deloitte, Haskins & Sells), pp. 81–98.

Flint, D. (1983) 'Dutch Accountancy: A Managerial Economics Based Approach', *The Accountant's Magazine,* July, pp. 267–8.

Gemmell, J.H.F. (1978) 'In Defence of Auditing Standards', *The Accountant's Magazine,* July, pp. 286–8.

Goerdeler, R. (1979) 'The International Federation of

Accountants', In J.W. Brennan (ed.), *The Internationalisation of the Accountancy Profession* (Toronto: CICA), pp. 5–13.

Goerdeler, R. (1981) 'International Practice: Auditing Standards and Quality Controls', in J.C. Burton (ed.), *The International World of Accounting: Challenges and Opportunities* (Reston, Virginia: The Council of Arthur Young Professors), pp. 155–76.

Gough, B. (1978) 'Just How Necessary are Auditing Standards?', *Accountancy*, July, p. 118.

Grojer, J. and A. Stark (1977) 'Social Accounting: A Swedish Attempt', *Accounting, Organizations and Society*, vol. 2, no. 4, pp. 349–86.

Hamilton, S. (1978) 'The Proposed Auditing Standards – A Personal View', *The Accountant's Magazine*, June, pp. 250–2.

Hood, N. and S. Young (1979) *The Economics of Multinational Enterprise* (London: Longman).

The Hundred Group (1981) *Audit: The Client's View* (London: The Hundred Group).

Institut der Wirtschaftsprüfer (1977) *Generally Accepted Standards for the Audit of Financial Statements, Generally Accepted Reporting Standards for the Audit of Financial Statements and Standards for the Issue of Audit Opinions* (Dusseldorf: IdW).

The Institute of Chartered Accountants in England and Wales (1961–79) *Statements on Auditing (U Series)* (London: ICAEW).

The Institute of Chartered Accountants in England and Wales (1976a) *Statutory Audit Requirements in the Netherlands* (London: ICAEW).

The Institute of Chartered Accountants in England and Wales (1976b) *Statutory Audit Requirements in Belgium* (London: ICAEW).

The Institute of Chartered Accountants in England and Wales (1977) *Requirements for Qualification as a Registeraccountant in the Netherlands* (London: ICAEW).

The Institute of Chartered Accountants in England and Wales (1978) *Professional Ethics for Registeraccountants in the Netherlands* (London: ICAEW).

The Institute of Chartered Accountants in England and Wales

(1980) *Requirements for Qualification as a Wirtschaftsprüfer in the Federal Republic of Germany* (London: ICAEW).

The Institute of Chartered Accountants in England and Wales (1983) *Guide to Professional Ethics* (London: ICAEW).

The Institute of Chartered Accountants of Scotland (1971–79) *Statements on Auditing (Series 3)* (Edinburgh: ICAS).

The Institute of Chartered Accountants of Scotland (1976) *Group Accounts – Reliance on Other Auditors* (Statements on Auditing no. 3/4) (Edinburgh: ICAS). (Also issued by ICAEW as Statement U21.)

The Institute of Chartered Accountants of Scotland (1980) *Auditing Standards and Guidelines* (Edinburgh: ICAS). (Also issued simultaneously by The Institute of Chartered Accountants in England and Wales, The Institute of Chartered Accountants in Ireland and The Association of Certified Accountants.)

International Accounting Bulletin (1983a) 'Australian NCSC Proposes Sweeping New Disclosures', *International Accounting Bulletin,* July, p. 8.

International Accounting Bulletin (1983b) 'Just What Are The International "Firms"?', *International Accounting Bulletin,* September, pp. 10–11.

International Accounting Bulletin (1983c) 'OECD Plans Summit for Top Standard-Setters', *International Accounting Bulletin,* October, p.1.

International Accounting Bulletin (1983d) 'AA Jumps to Top of World League', *International Accounting Bulletin,* December, pp. 1, 12 and 13.

International Federation of Accountants (1977) 'The Agreement and Constitution of the International Federation of Accountants' in J.W. Brennan, (ed.), *The Internationalisation of the Accountancy Profession* (Toronto: CICA).

International Federation of Accountants (1979) *Preface to International Auditing Guidelines of the International Federation of Accountants* (New York: IFAC).

International Federation of Accountants (1981) *Using the Work of Another Auditor* (International Auditing Guideline no. 5) (New York: IFAC).

Jack, R.B. (1983) 'Shareholder Protection and the Auditor', in

Symposium on Auditing Research (University of Glasgow).

Japanese Institute of Certified Public Accountants (1974) *Auditing Standards, Working Rules of Field Work, Working Rules of Reporting (Issued by the Business Accounting Deliberation Council, Ministry of Finance, Japan)* (Tokyo: JICPA).

Jensen, M.C. and W.H. Meckling (1976) 'Theory of the Firm: Managerial Behaviour, Agency Costs and Ownership Structure', *Journal of Financial Economics,* October, pp. 305–60.

Johnston, T.R., M.O. Jager and R.B. Taylor (1979) *The Law and Practice of Company Accounting* (4th edn) (Sydney: Butterworths).

Klaassen, J. (1980) 'Dutch Accounting Court: The Impact of the Enterprise Chamber on Financial Reporting in the Netherlands', *The Accounting Review,* April, pp. 327–41.

Krijgsman, P. (1982) 'When an International Firm isn't International', *Accountancy Age,* 29 April, p. 9.

Lafferty, M. and D. Cairns (1980) *Financial Times World Survey of Annual Reports 1980* (London: Financial Times Business Information Ltd).

Larson, R.E. (1983) 'Self-regulation: A Professional Step Forward', *Journal of Accountancy,* September, pp. 58–64.

Lee, T.A. (1972) *Company Auditing: Concepts and Practices* (London: Gee & Co).

Lee, T.A. and R.H. Parker (eds) (1979) *The Evolution of Corporate Financial Reporting* (Walton-on-Thames: Nelson).

Lessard, D.R. (1976) 'World, Country and Industry Relationships in Equity Returns: Implications for Risk Reduction Through International Diversification', *Financial Analysts Journal,* January–February, pp. 32–8.

Lothian, N. (1983) *Audit Quality and Value for Money* (Edinburgh: Heriot-Watt University).

McDougall, E.H.V. (1979) 'Regional Accountancy Bodies', in J.W. Brennan (ed.), *The Internationalisation of the Accountancy Profession* (Toronto: CICA), pp. 15–20.

Macharzina, K. (1981) 'Financial Reporting in West Germany', in Nobes and Parker (eds), *Comparative International Accounting* (Oxford: Philip Allan), pp. 123–59.

Macrae, E.W. (1981) 'Impediments to a Free International Market in Accounting and the Effects on International Accounting Firms', in J.C. Burton (ed.), *The International World of Accounting: Challenges and Opportunities* (Reston, Virginia: The Council of Arthur Young Professors).

Mantle, P. (1983) 'The French Revolution', *International Accounting Bulletin*, August, pp. 21–3.

Mason, A.K. (1978) *The Development of International Financial Reporting Standards* (ICRA Occasional Paper no. 17) (Lancaster: University of Lancaster).

Mason, R.H. (1974) 'Conflicts Between Host Countries and the Multinational Enterprise', *California Management Review*, Fall, pp. 5–14.

Mautz, R.K. and H.A. Sharaf (1961) *The Philosophy of Auditing* (Sarasota, Florida: American Accounting Association).

Mautz, R.K. (1975) 'The Role of Auditing in our Society', A Study Paper Prepared for the Commission on Auditors' Responsibilities (Cohen Committee).

Mead, G.C. (1980) 'The Accounting Profession in the 1980s – Some SEC Perspectives', in University of Kansas, *Auditing Symposium V: Proceedings of the 1980 Touche Ross/University of Kansas Symposium on Auditing Problems* (Kansas University).

Moir, J.A.W. (1980) 'The New Auditing Standards', *The Accountants' Magazine*, April, pp. 158–60.

Mueller, R. and E.G. Galbraith (1976) *The German Stock Corporation Law 1965 and The German Law on the Accounting by Major Enterprises other than Stock Corporations* (Frankfurt: Fritz Knapp Verlag).

Nederlands Instituut van Registeraccountants (NIVRA) (1972) *Act on Annual Accounts of Enterprises* (Amsterdam: *NIVRA*).

Nederlands Instituut van Registeraccountants (1977) *Rules of Conduct and Professional Practice of Registeraccountants* (Amsterdam: *NIVRA*).

Nobes, C.W. and R.H. Parker (1981) *Comparative International Accounting* (Oxford: Philip Allan).

OECD (1976) *Declaration on International Investment and Multinational Enterprises* (Paris: OECD).

OECD (1980) *International Investment and Multinational Enter-*

prises – Accounting Practices in OECD Member Countries (Paris: OECD).

Olson, W.E. (1980) 'Self-Regulation – What's Ahead?', *Journal of Accountancy,* March, pp. 46–9.

Parker, R.H. (1982) 'Company Legislation and Accounting Standards in Australia', *The Accountant's Magazine,* February, pp. 64–5.

Percival, C.T., P.J. Donaghy and J. Laidler (1982) *Glossary of European Accounting Charts* (Durham: Flambard (European)).

Perks, R.W. and R.H. Gray (1980) 'Social Accounting: The Role of the Accountant', *The Accountant's Magazine,* May, p. 201.

Picking, B.G. (1973) 'Auditing Standards', *Accounting and Business Research,* vol. 4, no. 13, Winter, pp. 60–70.

Pound, G. (1982) 'Auditing Standards Board Report', *The Chartered Accountant in Australia,* December, pp. 14–15.

Price Waterhouse International (1979) *International Survey of Accounting Principles and Reporting Practices* (Scarborough, Ontario: Butterworths).

Radford, R. (1980) 'Harmonisation of Company Law: Preparing for the Extra Burden', *Accountancy,* April, pp. 55–6.

Reckers, P.M.J. and A.J. Stagliano (1981) 'Non-Audit Services and Perceived Independence: Some New Evidence', *Auditing: A Journal of Practice and Theory,* Summer, pp. 23–37.

Reesor, L.J. (1978) 'Canada Examines the Role of the Auditor', *The Accountant's Magazine,* July, pp. 292–4.

Rentoul, J. (1982) 'Keeping Control in Partnership Around the World', *Accountancy Age,* 4 November, pp. 18–19.

Rentoul, J. (1983) 'Top Firm Attacks World Fee Figures', *Accountancy Age,* 10 February, p. 1.

Richards, W.R. (1976) 'Auditing US Companies with Operations Abroad', *International Journal of Accounting,* vol. 12, no. 1, pp. 1–11.

Sanders, P. (1977) *Dutch Company Law* (London: Oyez Publishing).

Savage, P. (1983a) 'What Future for Self-regulation?', *International Accounting Bulletin,* September, pp. 12–15.

Savage, P. (1983b) 'Radical Changes in the Accounting Business', *International Accounting Bulletin,* November, pp. 12–19.

Schoenfeld, H.W. (ed.) (1978) *The Status of Social Reporting in*

Selected Countries (Contemporary Issues in International Accounting, Occasional Paper no. 1) (Champaign-Urbana, Illinois: Centre for International Education and Research in Accounting).

Schoonderbeek, J.W., A. van Putten and J. Bloemarts (1980) *The Tripartite Accounting Standards Committee* (*NIVRA* Pilot Series No. 10) (Amsterdam: *NIVRA*).

Schreuder, H. (1978) *Facts and Speculations on Corporate Social Reporting in France, Germany and Holland* (Brussels: European Institute for Advanced Studies in Management).

Schreuder, H. (1981) 'Employees and the Corporate Social Report: The Dutch Case', *The Accounting Review*, April, pp. 294–308.

Sempier, R.N. (1979) 'The International Federation of Accountants: Operating Procedures and Current Progress', *International Journal of Accounting*, vol. 15, no. 1, pp. 21–31.

Shaw, J.C. (1980) *The Audit Report: What it Says and What it Means* (Edinburgh: ICAS).

Sherer, M. and D. Kent (1983) *Auditing and Accountability* (London: Pitman).

Shockley, R.A. (1981) 'Perceptions of Auditor Independence: An Empirical Analysis', *The Accounting Review*, October, pp. 785–800.

Skerratt, L.C.L. (1982) 'Auditing in the Corporate Sector: A Survey', in Bromwich, Hopwood and Shaw (eds), *Auditing Research: Issues and Opportunities* (London: Deloitte Haskins & Sells), pp. 69–79.

Skerratt, L.C.L. and D.J. Tonkin (1982) *Financial Reporting 1982–83: A Survey of UK Published Accounts* (London: ICAEW).

Solnik, B.H. (1974) 'Why Not Diversify Internationally?', *Financial Analysts Journal*, July–August, pp. 48–54.

Stamp, E. (1979) *The Future of Accounting and Auditing Standards* (ICRA Occasional Paper No. 18) (Lancaster: University of Lancaster).

Stamp, E. and M. Moonitz (1978) *International Auditing Standards* (London: Prentice-Hall International).

Standish, P. (1981) 'Financial Reporting in Britain and Australia', in Nobes and Parker, *Comparative International Accounting* (Oxford: Philip Allan), pp. 35–62.

The Times (1983) *The Times 1000 1983–4* (London: Times Books).

Tricker, R.I. (1980) *Corporate Accountability and the Role of the Audit Function* (Oxford: Corporate Policy Group).

Tripartite Accounting Standards Committee (1981) *Netherlands Accounting Guidelines* (Amsterdam: TASC).

UEC Auditing Statements Board (1978) *The Use of Another Auditor's Work* (Auditing Statement No. 2) (Munich: *UEC*).

United Nations Commission on Transnational Corporations (1977) *International Standards of Accounting and Reporting for Transnational Corporations* (New York: United Nations).

United Nations Commission on Transnational Corporations (1982) *Background Paper Discussing the Auditor's Association with Non-financial Information* (Working Paper no. 1982/6/3) (New York: United Nations).

University of Kansas (1980) *Auditing Symposium V: Proceedings of the 1980 Touche Ross/University of Kansas Symposium on Auditing Problems* (Kansas: University of Kansas).

Volten, H. (1979) 'Internationalisation – A National Perspective', in J.W. Brennan (ed.), *The Internationalisation of the Accountancy Profession* (Toronto: CICA).

Weinstein, A.K., L. Corsini and R. Pawliczek (1978) 'The Big Eight in Europe', *International Journal of Accounting*, vol. 13, no. 2, pp. 57–71.

Welchman, T. (1983) 'French Rules Inhibit Growth of Large, UK-style Firms', *Accountancy*, September, pp. 64–5.

Wirtschaftsprüferkammer (1981) *Law Regulating the Profession of Wirtschaftsprüfer, Examination Regulations for Wirtschaftsprüfer and Rules for the Professional Conduct of Wirtschaftsprüfer and Vereidigte Buchprüfer* (Dusseldorf: Wirtschaftsprüferkammer).

Woolf, E. (1979) *Auditing Today* (London: Prentice-Hall International).

Wu, F. and D.W. Hackett (1977) 'The Internationalisation of US Public Accounting Firms', *International Journal of Accounting*, vol. 12, no. 2, pp. 81–91.

Wysocki, K.V. (1983) 'Research into the Processes of Accounting Standard Setting in the Federal Republic of Germany', in

Bromwich, Hopwood and Shaw (eds), *Auditing Research: Issues and Opportunities* (London: Deloitte Haskins & Sells), pp. 57–67.

Zeff, S.A. (1979) 'Significant Developments in the Establishment of Accounting Principles in the United States, 1926–78', in Lee and Parker (eds) (1979), *The Evolution of Corporate Financial Reporting* (Walton-on-Thames: Nelson), pp. 208–21.

Zünd, A. (1983) 'Endeavours Towards the Harmonisation of Standards of Accounting and Reporting in the OECD and UNO: A Critical Appraisal', in M. Bromwich and A.G. Hopwood (eds), *Accounting Standards Setting: An International Perspective* (London: Pitman) pp. 106–20.

Index